A Year to Wellness

and Other

Weight Loss Secrets

Bertice Berry, PhD

FREEMAN HOUSE

Also by Bertice Berry

Redemption Song

The Haunting of Hip Hop

Jim and Louella's Homemde Heart Fix Remedy

When Love Calls, You Better Answer

I'm on My Way But Your Foot Is on My Head

Bertice: The World According to Me

Straight from the Ghetto. You Know You're Ghetto If....

You Still Ghetto

To Contact Us:

FreemanHousePublishing.Com

Ayearto.Com

ISBN 978-1-936683-00-0

For Christopher

Table of Contents

Acknowledgements

I HAVE MANY TO ACKNOWLEDGE AND MUCH TO BE grateful for.

I want to begin with the acknowledgement of my literary agent and friend of 17 years, Victoria Sanders. Victoria and her assistant Benee Knauer's belief in this project helped me to remain steadfast toward my goal for helping others in their journey to wellness.

My editor of 15 years and dear friend Janet Hill Talbert's contribution (and her beautiful jewelry at www.onthisrocknyc.com) helped me to move away from my anger towards the weight loss industry to a place of joy and celebration.

The newest member of my literary family, Tom Williams, PhD, has been a wealth of information and inspiration.

I am also grateful for my friends at Freeman Press, Jerry and Annette Lee for giving me tremendous courage in this new endeavor.

My wellness journey would not have been a success were it not for the wisdom of naturopath Mark Armstrong, massage therapist Christopher White, pediatrician Dr. Steven J. Hobby, and psychotherapist Randy Kasper and make-over genius, Pierra Lomedico of Piera's Salon.

I'd also like to acknowledge all of the beautiful folks who have joined me on this journey and have allowed me to use them as guinea pigs.

I am especially grateful to Adrianne Boner Dickey for being a beautiful and wise inspiration and true friend.

My wellness journey would not have been complete without the love and encouragement of the Rockingham family, Constance, Rocki and Tiphanie who has more photos of me than I do. Your encouragement is a blessing.

My sister Christine has loved me, prepared food and kept the children sane while I walked this beautiful journey. I am also grateful for her love and support throughout her own time of need when her son Christopher passed away. Her daily seven mile bike ride is an inspiration.

My sister/manager Jeanine Chambers has had to endure the journey and serve as typist as well. I am grateful to her for enabling me to test theories, try recipes and keep me laughing. Chupacabra!

I am eternally grateful for my youngest children, Fatima and Jabril for refusing to allow me popcorn, french fries or anything that didn't look healthy. I am inspired by their love and encouragement and for reminding me that life is all about choices.

And I acknowledge you the reader, who too often, has cared more for others than you have for yourselves. May you find all the joy that you deserve.

Preface

IN THE PAST, I'VE WRITTEN ABOUT SLAVERY, POVERTY, abuse and oppression. Somehow, I was able to do so while conveying a message of hope for the future. Writing a book about a weight loss journey then, should be—no pun intended—a piece of cake. It's been anything but.

When I first set out to write this book, I was angry. I was still raging about the weight loss industry and how it makes 56 billion dollars a year selling its snake oils and gimmicks to the desperate folks they've made fatter with potions, pills, surgeries and wacky programs. In the words of Malcolm X, we have been "Hoodwinked, bamboozled, led astray, run amok."

I was mad at those physicians who treat fat people unfairly and often fail to diagnose the illnesses and diseases that cause weight gain while telling us to "just push away from the table."

I was vexed with the media for portraying fat people as lazy, shiftless, dirty, ugly psychotics who are the cause of everything from their own poverty to the healthcare crisis.

And I was mad at two thirds of the American people who are classified as overweight or obese, for blaming themselves for being less than others simply because of how much they weigh. But most of all, I was angry with myself for not seeing all of this before.

I wanted to write a book that would shame those who have shamed us. So I did, and it was—well, shameful.

After reading and rereading, I came to see the powerful truth behind the old saying, "You can catch more flies with honey than you can with vinegar."

The Year to Wellness Plan has its foundation in forgiveness and gratitude; therefore, I needed to be grateful, and I had to forgive.

So I've scrapped the angry manuscript and re-placed it with one that reflects the place of joy and gratitude where I now live. The facts remain the same, but my perspective on them has changed, and I no longer have a need to bully the weight loss bullies.

This book tells the story of my journey toward complete wellness and outlines a plan for you to co-create your own journey.

As I have learned, you too will need to forget what you think you know about weight loss. You will have to open your mind and your heart to a whole new approach to being well in spirit, mind and body. You must come to see that losing weight is a result of getting well, not the other way around.

Be prepared to change from the inside out, and most of all, get ready to start loving *you*.

Introduction

IF YOU ASK ANYONE WHO HAS KNOWN ME FOR ANY length of time, they will tell you that I am a happy and confident woman. I have lived through hardship and abuse, but I've been determined to never become what was done to me.

Recently, while doing an interview on NPR radio about my Year to Wellness Program, the reporter asked how the program worked. I explained that it was not a quick fix or magic bullet, but required a whole year of gradual change in thoughts and behaviors and that it introduced basic wellness principals in a unique way.

The interviewer then asked how our listeners could get started.

"Well," I said with a little hesitation, "the first three days of the program require that the participant give themselves gratitude and forgiveness."

I explained that the individual would need to give thanks to their body for having carried their spirit, and that they would need to forgive themselves for not having fully loved who they are and how they look.

The silence was deafening. After a pause that felt way too long for radio, the interviewer retorted with something I had not anticipated. I had expected disbelief, doubt and even the suggestion that the plan was new age hooey. Instead the interviewer, whose show I'd been on several times before said, "Those of us who know and have listened to you have always thought that you were a confident woman who could see her own beauty."

The next second of silence was my own. In my mind I raced over my life, my looks, my presence, and I knew that what she said was accurate. I was and have been a confident, beautiful woman, but what she didn't know, what even my closest friends and family members were not aware of was this: I was not well.

I moved through life with the energy of a young bull, charging headlong into any obstacle in my way, but physically and emotionally my tank was near empty.

When you look at the pictures of me before I completed my wellness journey, you will see me smiling. The smile is real. It is not a façade, a mask to hide feelings of ugliness; it is me. Yet at the core of my being were old hurts and emotions that impacted my behavior, thoughts and ultimately my well-being.

The mind-body connection is real. What we think about and how we feel about those thoughts affects our health in many ways. This book will guide you through the program that has enabled me to erase hereditary disease and other illnesses resulting in the loss of 150 pounds. I did it slowly, gradually, easily, but it took a year. My results are amazing. My skin is tight and toned, lacking the look that most often accompanies large amounts of weight loss. My face appears as young as it did when I was in my twenties with one big difference; I have a brighter glow about me. I'm doing things I've never done, like wearing jeans and bikini bathing suits. I've given a solo dance performance in front of 8,000 people, and I sleep all night, every night, and most of all, I am well.

I recently saw a friend who I hadn't seen in 30 years. "My gosh, Bert," he said with his mid-western enthusiasm, "you've found the fountain of youth."

"Yes," I told him. "I have, and it's within me."

It is my sincere desire that you, too, will find the spark of the divine within you and that your light will illuminate a path towards wellness, truth, and love that others may follow.

Chapter One

The Way Out Is Way Back Through

*How I got over, over. My soul looks
back and wonders, how I got over.*
—*Negro Spiritual*

I'M NOT ONE OF THE MILLIONS OF AMERICANS WHO got fat later in life, nor did it happen as a result of childbirth. I am a mother to five children, but I did not give birth to them. I often joke about getting stretch marks the day they arrived. Four of my children are my maternal nieces and nephews and the other is the biological daughter of a childhood friend. There were no late night cravings, no morning sickness, and no pregnancy weight gain that never left. I was always fat.

As I have learned, so are lots of folks. Many of the fat Americans we see everyday are genetically predisposed to adiposity or in plain English, fat. But Western society fails to embrace this genetic diversity.

Only recently are Americans beginning to embrace ethnic and cultural diversity. We still have a great deal of difficulty tolerating religious differences and differences based on sexual orientation, but where weight is concerned, fat people are way down the list. Even fat people themselves have a hard time accepting the notion that we were not all born to be the same size.

No one would put on a size six shoe if they wore a size ten. They would not buy the shoe, take it home, placing it where it was visible, so that every time they saw it they could hope and pray that one day their size ten foot would become a six. We accept that the size ten is a ten and always will be. When it comes to our bodies though, we compare and contrast ourselves to others, looking for ways to be and feel better, only to end up feeling worse.

Our failure to embrace the fact that we are all different is the starting point of our weight and body image issues.

Think back to the period in time when you first

thought you were fat. If possible, find those old pho-tos of your so-called "fat days." More likely than not, you will see the same thing I did, the same thing most people do, that you were not fat. If you are bru-tally honest with yourself, you'll have to admit that you are and were beautiful and that there was noth-ing wrong with you to begin with. Somehow though, you—as I did—thought you were less than perfect, so you started on a cycle of losing and gaining and losing and gaining.

Research shows, that people who diet and lose weight, gain back an average of 10 pounds or more in addition to the amount they originally lost. Still, we go back to that diet plan or the next latest and greatest, hoping to get different results. **(It has often been said that the definition of insanity is doing the same thing over and over again, expecting different results.)**

Diets don't work because they are based on de-privation. When you deprive your body of what it needs, you cannot assist it in healing itself, which, as you will learn, it is designed to do.

My own weight gain started when I accepted

someone else's perception of me as a banner for my existence. In 1969, Louis Marx Toys had just introduced their new Big Wheel bike at the annual New York Toy Fair. The Big Wheel was the bright red, blue and yellow plastic low-to-the-ground three wheeled "king of the sidewalk." It became an immediate success. Every kid wanted one, and if you were lucky, middle class, or cried long enough, you got your wish. I was a poor kid with a mother who did not believe in tantrums, so at age nine I watched as other kids raced their Big Wheels into impressive spins and turns.

Calvin, the boy who lived down the street from my family, was one of the first kids in the neighborhood to get a Big Wheel. He and my older brother Kevin were buddies and often shared their homemade go-carts and reassembled bikes. Calvin showed up one Christmas morning with his brand new Big Wheel, and Kevin and I couldn't wait for a chance to ride.

We lived on Gordon Street, which was wedged between Twenty-second and Twenty-third streets in Wilmington, Delaware. Gordon Street was more of an alley than a street, so few cars ever drove up and down the block, making it the perfect place for barefoot races, go-cart maneuvers and now Big Wheel gatherings.

That Christmas, Calvin was joined by others who took turns pushing the Big Wheel as fast as possible. After the bike reached maximum speed, the pusher would impressively jump on the back of the seat and speed down the road until the *pushee* spun out into an exhilarating twirl followed by an abrupt stop.

I watched the other kids go back and forth in anticipation of my turn on the Big Wheel, but it never came. When I asked Calvin for a ride, he looked at me and laughed. "You can't ride my Big Wheel." He said it loud enough for all the other kids to hear.

"My mother said that the directions say you can't be over 100 pounds and you are fat," he said laughing.

I could not speak, nor could I think fast enough to realize that surely he and my brother together exceeded the weight restrictions. It was the 1960s, and I already had the insecurity that came with being poor and black, so I had no way of giving Calvin the

proverbial piece of my mind. Instead, I looked dumb-
ly at him and said, "I'm not that big." That was all I
could muster. My brother Kevin, who up until that
moment had been my best friend, my ace, my sidekick, picked up Calvin's cause and started to chant,

"I'm not that big, but I'm a pig. I'm not that big,
but I'm a pig."

I was humiliated. For the next eight years of
my life, Kevin called me Pig or "Gip" which was pig
spelled backwards.

Needless to say, the Big Wheel event and all of
the other fat-identifying incidents that followed had
an impact.

When I was twelve, I was told that I was obese.
This was the early seventies when public schools had
registered nurses who served as community health
care providers and performed the check-ups and
necessary vaccinations for poor and underinsured
children.

"Jump on the scale," the school nurse said to me
the day of my exam. She muttered something that
sounded like, "*If* you can jump."

I grew up with six brothers and sisters, so name

calling or "playing the dozens" as we called it, was like breathing air. I had already endured my brother's taunt, so the nurses' comment was like an annoying song playing in the background; it bothers you but you learn to ignore it.

The nurse was short and squat and reminded me of a female version of the cartoon characters Elmer Fudd and Mr. Magoo. I resisted the urge to ask the nurse about *her* high jump record and got on the scale.

"Tsk, tsk, tsk." She muttered and shook her head.

"Just as I thought," she said. "You are obese," she said, dragging the word out for what felt like an eternity: "Ooooooooooooo---beeeeeeeeeeeeeeeeeese."

She went on to say that if I didn't stop eating so much, I would become very sick and might die before I reached the age of forty.

I was only twelve years old, but I was being told that overeating would be the cause of my death. Back then, my family was extremely poor, so we hardly ever had enough to eat and we certainly didn't have enough to overeat. Little was known about the impact of genetics on adiposity and even less was understood about the connection between improper nourishment and weight gain. All the nurse knew was that I was fat, and I was unhealthy.

Armed with even less information than the nurse had, I went to my favorite place on earth, the public library, and searched for ways to prevent my "untimely death." After attempting to read several unreadable diet books, I found an article about vegetarianism. It pointed out that vegetarians were healthier and lived longer than heavy meat eaters.

My mother had grown up on a farm with her grandparents who mainly ate the vegetables they grew, so we ate vegetables too. On the rare occasions when meat was served, I found it hard to digest and often got sick from the Thanksgiving or Christmas turkey or the Easter ham.

I decided that being a vegetarian would be easy, so at the young age of thirteen, I made the choice to do without meat. There was still the occasional piece of fried chicken or tuna sandwich, but for the most part, I was a vegetarian.

What I ate in the place of meat, however, did little for weight loss. While I avoided the Thanksgiving turkey, I learned to make a meal out of the stuffing, sweet potatoes and macaroni and cheese that often accompanied holiday dining. Desserts were rare in my household, so when friends invited me over and offered them to me, I jumped at the opportunity to discover the wonders of sugar.

With a diet of very little protein but large amounts of sugar, I somehow avoided the diabetic condition that many in my family suffered from; still I was just at the beginning of the many trials and errors I'd make before becoming healthy.

When it was time for my senior prom, a boy named Michael (his last name is omitted but not forgotten) invited me to go with him. On the night of the prom, Michael didn't show up. I called him and discovered that he had no intentions of taking me; that his invitation had been a joke. He said that he was not going to be seen with a fat girl. Instead of going to the prom I spent the night with a big bowl of popcorn mixed with M&Ms.

When I look back on all of these events, I now realize that I was not fat. In fact, the size I was then was the initial goal I set for myself when I started my Wellness Program. The stigma and stereotyping I experienced in my youth were just the beginning of what society would have in store for me.

After graduating from high school, my talent, smarts, and several exceptional educators helped me to go to college, but again I faced the discrimination that comes with weight. At Jacksonville University, in Jacksonville, Florida, even the skinny people thought they were fat.

J. U. was and is an amazing learning environment. I was surrounded by people from all over the world who were eager to learn and ready to share what they knew. I was exposed to the wide range of diversity in people and in thought. But I also experienced the narrow-mindedness that comes with weight bias.

I joined the show choir (a choral group like the one on the television show "*Glee*" that does dance moves while singing) and was shocked by the ridicule of audience members who laughed out loud when I approached the microphone. But as I opened my mouth to sing, the powerful gospel tones and phrases took over and I was rewarded with standing ovations. I had learned to turn preconceived ideas into praise and I loved every moment of it. Still, at the end of a successful year for the show choir, the director, a fat man, informed me that even though I had been the star of the choir, I could not come back unless I lost weight, which, he informed me, was distracting people from my talent.

I was angry and embarrassed, but I did not confront him. I wanted to ask what my weight had to do with my ability to sing. I wanted to know if he was going to hold himself to the same standards and if he had a magic pill for weight loss, but I said none of this. I walked away and decided that I would show him what I could do.

That summer, I starved myself and exercised so much that I lost eighty pounds. I looked incredible. Old friends didn't recognize me and everyone wanted my secret.

At the end of the summer, I passed out while playing racquetball and ended up in the hospital. After a week of being treated for malnutrition and severe dehydration, I was invited back to show choir and even asked to represent several organizations in the University's upcoming pageant. I said no to show choir. I had achieved weight loss success at the cost of my health, but no one cared about the price I had paid. I looked great, and that was all that mattered.

During my years in graduate school I maintained weight loss through rigorous exercise and body building. The strenuous workouts fit nicely with my rigid academic discipline and provided the much needed breaks from demanding research.

A few years after finishing my doctoral degree, I had become an entertainer and lecturer and soon landed a nationally syndicated television talk show, *The Bertice Berry Show* (1991-1992). Now, in case you haven't already heard, television is said to add ten pounds, but I know from experience that the stress from television executives actually adds about fifty. Just before the show launched, my sister Myrna, who had always been my biggest cheerleader, died from complications of diabetes and alcoholism. My sadness went unnoticed, but the sudden drop in weight (a result of grieving,) was viewed positively and even encouraged.

One day, while I was hosting the television

show, I was instructed by the shows executives to watch the viewer focus group research video tapes. I was informed that it was necessary to improve my performance as a host. I watched with members of my staff and television executives as the participants in the focus groups were asked to discuss what they thought of me and the show. The initial overall reaction was extremely positive with viewers stating that they loved the show and felt that I was a well-informed and lively host. As the questioning of the focus group continued, the interviewer moved in closer to the subjects and asked them what they thought of my looks and particularly my body. Again the participants responded positively saying that they thought I was a confident and beautiful woman who seemed to be "happy with herself and in her own skin."

Not being satisfied with these answers, the interviewer moved in closer still, and in an authoritative voice asked the participants if they thought I should lose weight since I was on television representing African Americans and women. I watched in shock when another thirty minutes of this line of drilling continued. Eventually, the participants, women aged

20-45, relented and began to make disparaging remarks.

"She *has* gained a lot of weight since she first came on television," one woman commented. Another said that she felt that I represented the stereotyped image of the loud, big butt black woman. After watching more than two hours of these focus group tapes, I was asked, in front of my staff, what I thought about the interviews and what *I* specifically could do to make the show better.

I should have reminded the executives that I had a PhD in sociology with an emphasis in research analysis and stratification (the unequal distribution of wealth and power in a society.) I should have said that I was painfully aware of the fact that the conversations were coerced and the result of a deliberate attempt to get the focus group participants to point out what the executives wanted them to say—that I was fat. I should have informed the television executives that research could be used to prove or disprove the same event. And I should have told that group of all male executives that by their own standards, they too were fat and therefore unattractive. Instead,

I said nothing.

Shortly afterwards, I went back to my old pattern of starving and over exercising. At the time of this event, I weighed between 145-155 pounds. Years later when I ballooned up to 290 pounds I looked back at pictures and tapes from that period and realized how small I really was.

A few years ago, and thirty five years after I first heard that I was "obese," I heard the same thing again. This time though, it was coming from a successful cardiologist. The physician was also rather stout and much shorter than I am. (I'm only 5'3".)

"You need to have gastric bypass surgery." He proclaimed. After a quick examination, he said that my health issues were becoming more and more serious and that my weight had been the cause of them all.

"You need to do something fast." He said, "Or things will only get worse."

I had no intention of undergoing any form of what I perceived to be unnecessary surgery. At the time, I weighed 250 pounds and I had thought of gastric bypass as a last resort surgery for people who weighed more than 500 pounds. When I told the physician this, he said that the surgery was being done on people who weighed even less than I did and that they were now living healthy lives. I knew that it wasn't as easy as he made it sound.

A few years before this, I had been interviewed on a radio show that dealt with the topic of bariatric surgery. I learned that while there were many bariatric success stories, there were far too many stories that ended in death.

According to the Slim America Weight Loss Project (2007), ten to twenty percent of the people who undergo weight loss surgery have serious complications. Over ten percent of people with complications actually die.

Bariatric surgery or weight loss surgery includes gastric bypass, stomach stapling, laparoscopic surgery, gastroplasty and liposuction. The side effects of bariatric surgery include nausea and vomiting, dehydration, food intolerance, weight regain and death.

I had no intention on gambling with my life. I felt that at 250 pounds I had a greater chance of losing weight on my own. I preferred not losing weight and living to the risk of death from weight loss surgery.

When I moved from California to Georgia, the cost of medical insurance skyrocketed. I decided to try a plan that claimed to have better coverage at a lower cost. When the nurse arrived at my house to do a routine physical, she could barely make it up the steps of my southern-style home. The house is pitched high to take advantage of cool breezes and marsh and river views. She panted and complained and asked for a glass of water before she could get on with her tasks.

During this time, my 87-year-old mother suffered from several serious illnesses, including a brain tumor and a series of strokes and heart attacks. I had been caring for her along with my children. I knew that I had been more stressed than usual, but I wanted to keep the appointment as I was never sure what condition my mother might be in. The nurse took my blood pressure and informed me that it was slightly high and once again, I was informed that I was "obese."

Before my weigh-in, I had asked the nurse to take

my weight without telling me what it was, as scales tended to stress me even more. She said that she understood, but as I stood on the scale, eyes closed for my own protection, the nurse loudly announced that I weighed 228 pounds. My children and boyfriend at the time were in earshot of her declaration. I should have been happy.

According to her scale I had lost 22 pounds since my last doctor's visit, but I could hear my son as he let out a whistle and my boyfriend as he told him to be quiet. The nurse then said that she was amazed, since I looked smaller than she did and I had to agree. She went on to tell me that she had had bariatric surgery and had lost 100 pounds. I wanted to tell her that she should ask for her money back, but I just smiled and said congratulations. She told me that I should have the surgery and that the insurance company would probably deny me coverage due to my height and weight ratio and the fact that my blood pressure was slightly elevated. I informed her that my blood pressure was always fine, but that this had been a very stressful week. She smiled and told me to get the surgery, that I would be happy that I did.

A week later, I got a call from someone in the insurance company who asked if I had ever considered bariatric surgery. I told the woman no and said that I had already started to lose weight on my own. Later on, I was informed by letter that I could not be covered at my current weight. I went back to my old insurance company at an even higher premium.

Later that year, my mother passed away. I missed her company and the love she shared with me and my children. I became even more stressed, and my weight got up to 290 pounds.

My doctor told me that I was depressed and that my weight had caused other health issues. He said that unless I did something quickly, I'd be joining my mother in heaven.

I was thinking, "Really nice bedside manner, Doc." He prescribed a series of pills, reiterated the need for surgery and told me to make time in my schedule for the operation.

After caring for my mother, my five adopted children and touring all over the country teaching other people to love themselves and the work they did, I found that I had spent very little time on me. I suffered from several serious illnesses and needed more medial coverage. Again I tried to increase the coverage by switching policies, and again I was declared "uninsurable" because of "obesity." I ran back to my old provider and looked for ways to get healthy.

I started on a journey of wellness that was soon derailed when one of the children I raised died tragically at the age of eighteen. The loss of a child is devastating for any parent; I was no different. Every obstacle became a roadblock on my journey to wellness.

Then my nephew Christopher, who was forty-two years old, died of a massive stroke brought on by undiagnosed hypertension. Christopher's death became a real wake up call. Instead of it being an excuse to eat badly and skip meals, Christopher's passing became my reason to do the right thing. I started by researching diets and fitness programs to find the one that would best suit my busy, vegetarian lifestyle. I soon learned that there was no one program designed just for me. I then looked through research findings and holistic materials for a plan of attack.

Good information was everywhere. It was scattered all over like a long lost treasure with clues, hither and yon, waiting for some deserving adventurer to bring them together and unlock the puzzle of pain and suffering.

As I started out, I knew that I had to redefine what a healthy body would look and feel like.

I had been raised on the anorexic images that filled magazine pages and even looked too thin on the television and cinema screens. I had been judged by the unrealistic weight charts which indicated that I should be around 124 pounds, even though I looked and felt better between 140 and 160 pounds.

I soon came to understand that weight, like everything else about the human body was linked to genetics and is as unique and varied as our genes. I learned that true wellness, not the number on a scale, was the real prize.

After a great deal of research which continues even now, I redefined wellness from a more holistic perspective as **the realignment of the spirit or energy with the mind and body.** I had spent years developing my mental and spiritual life, but had left my body behind. It was time to wake it up, to realign it with my mind and spirit. I have a picture of myself singing in front of a choir. In the picture, I am wearing a fancy beaded skirt and cashmere sweater that is also adorned with sequins and beads. My dreadlocks are pulled back into a neat ponytail and my makeup is flawless. In the picture, I am performing with a group of people from The International Spa Association at their annual conference. We are singing a song I wrote called *You Are Beautiful*. The lyrics are simple*: "You are beautiful, you are wonderful, you are powerful, just as you are, just as you are."* In this picture, I weigh 290 pounds; I am larger than everyone else. Still, I was able to see my beauty and strength.

The beginning of any life change must start in the mind. When I first saw that picture, I was shocked by how large I had become. I was the old fat show choir singer, but this time, nobody was laughing. The audience loved the song and me from start to finish. I had changed people's thinking and perception of me, but now it was time to change *me*.

I decided to give myself at least a year to "get well," and soon noticed that my wellness plan had a life of its own. The pounds seemed to drop off ,and my physical exams were improving rapidly.

I was thinking, moving and sleeping much better. I bought my very first pair of jeans two sizes too small and watched in amazement as they soon fit and then quickly became too big. I discussed my Wellness Plan with no one, looking instead to books and my own mind's eye for inspiration.

There is an ancient proverb that says, **"When a person seeks their purpose, the Universe conspires to make it happen."**

This is what happened with my Wellness Plan; I went looking for wellness and it happened. *By* **combining proper nutrition, well balanced exercise, massage therapy, proper rest and hydration with visualization, mediation and sleep therapy, I have enabled my body to heal itself.** I have learned to love and embrace the thick thighs that have carried me and to be grateful for my large round behind that never let my back down. As I have shown love to my entire body, it has rewarded me with good health. The journey has not been easy, but it has been beautiful, wonderful and powerful. Now I love me just as I am, just as I am.

Reflections and Exercises

AT THE END OF each chapter, you will find a series of reflections and exercises. They will enable you to reflect on your own experiences before, during and after your Year To Wellness. Read the book through in its entirety before answering the questions. When you do, be as honest and as thorough as possible. Use the blank space provided, and when necessary, keep an additional journal used solely for the purpose of your Year to Wellness. And remember: "An unexamined life is not worth living."

In the previous pages, I have outlined my own road to being "un-well." Tell your story. Describe several events that made you feel badly about yourself and your body.

When did you first learn or come to believe
that you were fat?

How has your weight impacted your life
and the choices you have made?

Describe how you would like to feel
and look in one year.

Notes

"When you walk with Purpose,
you collide with Destiny"

Chapter Two

What I Did For Love

"When we are no longer able to change a situation,
we are challenged to change ourselves."
—*Physician and Holocaust survivor, Victor Frankl*

BEFORE I CAN TELL YOU ABOUT MY ROAD TO WELL-ness success, I feel that I need to be brutally honest with you about my wellness failures. Like most fat people, I initially thought that my health issues were a result of the weight gain that was caused by my lack of will power and gluttony. Even though I am vegetarian and always exercised regularly, I was still fat.

Late one night when I couldn't sleep, I saw an infomercial for a meal plan that could even work with the vegetarian diet. I thought, "Great, there are others like me." I ordered the meal plan, had it shipped by overnight delivery (which cost an additional seventy-six dollars) and got started on it right away. Within the first three days, I lost 11 pounds. I would later learn that I'd lost water weight, but 11 pounds was an amazing start. Any first year marketing student will tell you that if you want to sell a product that is supposed to create some kind of change, then you must be able to demonstrate immediate change and support it with success stories. When I heard the tearful stories of the people on the infomercial and saw the dramatic before and after pictures, I said exactly what the advertisers wanted me to say, "If they can do it, I can too."

I told anyone who would listen that they should order the product right away. The meal plan included a web site with even more before and after pictures and chat rooms where people could encourage each other online. There were rooms for single mothers, men, and people over 50. There were chat rooms based on location and there were chat groups for those who followed the tips of their favorite before and after stories and some for people who weighed themselves on a specific day of the week. If you missed a group, you could read their posted blogs. I joined in, and at first, I experienced the same high my chat room buddies did. We encouraged one another to stay away from picnics and barbeques, and to just say no when cookies came around. Someone always had creative ways to make cookies from the diet shake mix (they were awful) or protein bars from packages of oatmeal. When I felt weak and ready to quit, I'd go to the before and after photos of "successful" people for inspiration.

After about five weeks, I noticed something odd. Of the hundreds of thousands of folks who were said to be users of the products, the chat rooms always had the same 8 to 15 people. I also noticed that there were hardly any new success photos. I wondered how so many people could be using the product, with few talking about their success. Then the chat rooms that had been buzzing with enthusiasm started to sound like a complaint forum. I'm almost always optimistic, but even I began to lose faith in the product. The prices seemed to be getting higher, while the delivery was slower. Packages were lost, orders not processed, and the food which I found bearable at first began to leave me feeling bloated. Then I noticed that I was either constipated or had excessive gas at the most inopportune times. I wanted to find out if I was alone in my struggle, so I went to a chat room and posed a question, "Anyone in here having bowel problems?"

The chat room lit up with activity. There were stories of constipation, gas and even diarrhea. People reported constant headaches, leg cramping and difficulty with urination. I understood that many of the problems could have been a result of preexisting conditions. I also knew that there could be a "me too" factor at work that made others in the chat room want to join in the chorus.

But the similarities were too much to ignore. Still, I continued with the meal program but with modifications. I added more fiber to my diet and drank more water. With my heavy travel schedule, bathroom logistics were always difficult. I was constantly running to find bathrooms and praying that I would make it there in time. The bathroom situation was bad enough, but I also had to try to mix dry powdered shakes while in airports and prepare microwaveable meals in hotels. I decided to eat on my own. I would eat low calorie meals more regularly instead of the prepackaged meals. As soon as I did though, the weight I had lost (at least 30 pounds) came rushing back and it brought friends. I gained 50 pounds in a little over two and a half months.

I later learned that when our body loses weight suddenly, our metabolism responds by slowing down, enabling us to preserve the energy we have left. I had been in starvation mode, eating only 700 to 800 calories per day. When I fed my body food, any food, it packed on the pounds as quickly as possible in an attempt to replace what had been lost.

When Kirstie Alley lost 70 pounds on a food program, she proudly paraded her new figure in a bikini for millions of viewers on the Oprah Winfrey Show. The diet company's stock went up, and all was well with the world. But when Kirstie gained even more weight than she originally started at, she was ceremoniously dumped. The same folks who saw a huge profit and increase in clients, immediately sent out a press release stating that Ms. Alley was no longer a representative of their product. (They didn't even send her a goodbye package of food.)

Sadly, Kirstie Alley went *back* on Oprah to apologize. Kirstie is not alone in the cycle of losing and replacing weight[1]. Research shows that over 75% of people who lose weight on diet programs replace and gain more weight. (UCLA Magazine, 2007)

The winner of the third season of the television show, "The Biggest Loser", Erik Chopin lost a whopping 214 pounds but fell into depression after the show and gained back 122 pounds. Erik, who said he felt that he let everybody down, blamed the replacement weight on the fact that he felt bad when he stopped getting the attention he had gotten from winning the show. In his mind, the weight gain had nothing to do with the way he lost weight— an unrealistic eight hour a day, rigorous exercise regime and strictly monitored diet. Instead, he felt that the weight replacement was his fault entirely.

When we lose weight, we praise the diet industry, but when we gain or replace weight, we blame ourselves. We have become the biggest losers, while the weight loss industry wins big.

---

1 We will discuss the concept of replacement *weight* in a later chapter.

After my bout with prepackaged processed meal plans, it dawned on me that eating too much food was not my issue. As a vegetarian with a hectic travel schedule, I hardly ate at all. It didn't occur to me to try to eat more. It would take several more months to recognize that eating more throughout the day would help keep my metabolism running like the fine-tuned machine it was designed to be. Instead I grabbed on to the other popular notion about weight loss—exercising more. I remembered back when I'd lost weight in college. I had exercised excessively and been able to lose weight quickly. I chose to ignore how sick I had become as a result and focused on how good I looked during that period of time.

At the end of my junior year in college, I exercised as much as most professional athletes. So at 47, I decided that I would go back to the weight lifting, racquetball, swimming and running that I did when I was 19.

Planning and preparing the activities actually lasted longer than the activities themselves. It took even less time for me to come to a major realization;

I was no longer 19. Still like most people I jumped back into exercise like I'd been doing it everyday. My spirit was willing, but my flesh was terribly weak.

I drove to a gym to walk on a treadmill. I took one look at all of the skinny people in tight biker shorts and little midriff tops and wanted to run from the place. I decided to go to a Pilates class instead. The twenty-something waif at the reception desk tried hard to stifle her laughter as I tried hard to jog up to the desk. My arms were pumping as fast as they could, but my legs were barely moving, and that movement was causing a great deal of friction between my thighs. I got to the young woman and asked her about the Pilates class I had seen on their website. She snickered and informed me that the next class was advanced, "It's not for beginners," she said, looking me up and down. I wanted to tell her that I had already done the beginners course, but was afraid she ask when and where, and I'd have to tell her years ago at home with a DVD. Instead, I asked what other classes were starting soon. She asked if I had a membership and when I said no, she lit up and suddenly became enthusiastic.

"Oh, let me call a personal trainer for you," she said, with a big grin. She looked over a schedule and smiled even brighter.

"You are sooooooo lucky. John, *(not his real name)* is open right now. He's never open; you'll love him."

She grinned and paged John to the front desk, still smiling about something she said I wouldn't regret.

"He's the best," she promised. "He'll have you slim in no time."

Part of me wanted to smack her for pointing out that I wasn't slim, but a bigger part of me wanted to hug her for what she promised would be a gift.

Within moments, John jogged in. (He really could jog.) Muscles rippled and rolled as this 6'4" specimen came up to meet me. John had a beautiful smile, but what really set my heart at ease was his cologne. It had an intelligent smell. Don't ask me how cologne can make you smell smart, but somehow John's did. One whiff of his fragrance told me that he would know just what I needed to get in shape.

"Hey, beautiful," he purred. He exchanged pleasantries with the woman at the front desk, but I didn't understand much of it. I was basking in the compliment. As John led me to a small, glassed-in room, he offered me something to drink. I declined, and we went in. "Sheila says you are new, no membership, right?" he asked. I told him that I just wanted to take a Pilates class, but Sheila had informed me that it was just for advanced students. "Yeah, she can be like that sometimes." Then he said something that made him as smart as he smelled. "She's too skinny for my taste; I like a woman with meat on her bones. There's nothing like a big girl," he smiled.

Well, I thought, I was going to love this place.

John went on to say that while I looked good to him, I still needed to be at my best fitness level and that he was just the person who could get me there. He told me that he hadn't planned on taking any new clients as his schedule was pretty full, but he was interested in seeing what he could do for my body. Without missing a beat, he pulled out a contract and started listing the things that I would need to have done—weight, body mass index resting heart rate, things I didn't care to comprehend. The more he talked, the more I knew this would cost, so I cut in and asked about an introductory offer.

"Is there something that will allow me to try a class to see if I like it before I sign up for the whole deal?"

In a split second, John's façade faded and he looked as if he would ask me to leave. He pursed his lips and let out the smallest sigh, but then just as quickly changed back into the man who had called me beautiful.

John smiled his best smile and said, "There is an introductory package, yes." He looked around as if checking to see if anyone was listening and then laid it on real good.

"That package has all kinds of fine print. You'll end up paying whether you come in or not," he said in a whisper.

"I'd rather you take a full six month package with me training you three times a week—and more if you'd like—and then you can go from there, I know I can make you even more beautiful."

Suddenly, old John's cologne started to stink and I felt that I was being reeled in to a boat I didn't want to be on.

I'd heard stories from friends about paying for fitness programs they didn't want to use. I'd even read reports about how some fitness centers were like crooked landlords renting the same space over and over to folks who saw an apartment in the daylight, only to find that at night the place was unlivable.

With some contracts there's no getting out of the deal. You have to keep paying even though they rent that space to someone else.

I'd also heard stories about trainers who turned into angry drill sergeants, yelling insults and orders until clients became fatigued, sick and even dehydrated. One friend told me that her trainer made her feel like a failure when she didn't make "his" weight loss goals.

All of that went running though my mind as John sat there with his contract and his now-suffocating cologne. John was tapping his pen on his clipboard to hurry my response.

"Can I take this home and think about it?" I asked. You would have thought I had called John a pencil-necked weakling.

He jumped up from his seat and headed for the

door. "I really don't have time for this," he said.

"I've already told you, my schedule is full. Everybody wants to work out with me, even the other trainers. I was trying to do you a favor, you being a sister and all."

I was trying to take all of this in. I had gone from beautiful to just black. John hesitated for a second, hoping I would stop him from leaving. When I didn't he came back in on his own. "Look," he said, "Why don't I give you a session and you decide."

Something in me said, "Don't do it," but something else said "Just try it." I wanted to see what he could do in one session that would be so amazing, and so I said okay. I'll spare you the lengthy details and get right to it. I've already told you that I worked out in college. I told John too. He took that piece of advice and ran with it. He encouraged me and told me how much better I was than any client he'd ever trained. With my stamina and strength he'd have me fit in no time. We would be a perfect team.

Sadly for John, he'd never get to find out. At the end of the session, I told him I still wanted to think about it, and he informed me that he wouldn't be able to wait for my decision. Someone else wanted his empty time slot, but he'd told them no. Now, he was just going to allow that person to have it. I thanked him and left knowing that I made the right decision. Amazingly, John called me the next day and the one after that. He told me that he'd thought about it and he wanted to give me a second chance.

Wow, I thought to myself, all this and we weren't even dating.

John did something for me, more than he could know. While he was trying to sell me a package by telling me how good I was, he encouraged me to believe that I could be fit on my own. I just needed to take the time to do it.

I decided to exercise in the privacy of my own home. I already had a swimming pool, so I transformed a small room in my garage into a home gym. I bought all the necessary equipment: weights, benches, an elliptical trainer, and even an inversion board. I had a professional mirror maker come in to measure the front wall so I could have a floor-to-ceiling mirror to watch my workouts and progress. When the room was done, I was ecstatic. Now I would get the results I needed right at home.

I put on my workout clothes and went to the gym singing Michael Jackson's *Man in the Mirror.*

I sang as I got on the elliptical for a little cardio warm up. Not wanting to admit my weight even to myself, I punched in a fake weight, and a low-level workout program and got started. I covered up the panel with my towel so I wouldn't focus on the time as it went down.

I'd decided to start slowly. In my peak workout days, I could do 45 minutes and still lift weights. I had set the elliptical to 20 minutes and started my climb to fitness. After working and sweating hard, I removed the towel wondering why the timer hadn't gone off. I was feeling the pain, so I should have been over or at least close to twenty minutes. I had done a full 5 minutes and 40 seconds. I figured the elliptical was broken, so I looked at the clock my son had hung and saw that it too had barely moved. I made a mental note to tell my son he had forgotten to put a battery in. I decided that I'd stay on the elliptical a little longer, but when it read six minutes, I was done. I got off and tried to catch my breath before it left my body. I got dizzy. I was in worse shape than I'd originally thought. I looked at myself in the huge mirror and wanted to break it with one of my new dumbbells. Sweat was actually pouring off of my body and I appeared much fatter than I had before.

Not wanting my family to think I was a quitter, I decided to wait a while before going back up the stairs to face them. I sat down on the floor and actually fell asleep. (Did I mention that I had put in special gym flooring?)

I was curled up in a puddle of drool and sweat when my family came and found me. They lovingly took me back upstairs, where I decided to stay.

My son loves his home gym.

Exercise is good, necessary and can be done at home, but it should be done sensibly and chosen carefully, like one chooses a spouse—make sure it's something you really like so that you'll stay with it when the love wears off.

Think back over your attempts to lose weight, get fit and be well. Do any stand out as ridiculous or funny? Find a way to laugh about the situation and share it with a friend.

Have you ever been made to feel less than
wonderful by someone who's job it was
to help you be better? Forgive and let go of the past.

Do you enjoy exercise?
Think of an activity you love and would like to do again.

Write out a plan for doing it, but don't start until
after you've read the entire book.

Notes

"When you walk with Purpose,
you collide with Destiny"

Chapter Three

I've Fallen and I Can't Get Up

"I felt about exercise the same way that I feel about
a few other things: that there is nothing wrong with it
if it is done in private
by consenting adults."
—*Anna Quindlen*, Living Out Loud

AFTER MY FAILED ATTEMPT AT GETTING BACK into exercise with a trainer and then on my own, I decided that what I really needed was what I called "family fun fitness;" activities I could do with friends and family members while having fun. I called a friend who, like me had been a racquetball fanatic in her youth and who was also physically unfit. She was as excited as I was about having some sister-girl time while getting a workout.

It took us a few weeks before we actually made

it to the racquetball court, but when we got there, we were like two young girls. The sweaty smell, the shiny wooden floors, and the sound of our voices booming off the enclosed four walls brought back memories of a more active youth. We spent the first 15 minutes warming up our game and trash-talking skills.

"I hope you paid up your insurance this month, because I'm sending you to the doctor." My friend said. She lobbed a ball lightly to the front wall and then returned her own serve.

"Yeah, well you better call your husband and tell him to start running a tub of hot water because you are going to be sore for a week," I said laughing.

We laughed and trash-talked until we figured we were warmed up. Old memories of being the best racquetball player on campus came rushing back, but my body couldn't keep up the thoughts. I swerved and reached backwards like Keanu Reeves in *The Matrix* and connected with the high speed serve my friend sent flying at me. I gave the ball the momentum and speed it needed to arch high and then drop into the kill shot I had been known for in college. My friend, who had bragged about her hustle, dove racquet first towards the shot, expecting to slide under it just in time to save the ball and keep it in play. Instead of sliding, though, she fell and just stopped. As the ball bounced in front of her she inched slowly forward, laughing the whole time. Her body squeaked as she did; inch, squeak, inch, squeak, inch, squeak. Still aching from my Matrix move, I fell to the floor and laughed with her. We were still laughing when we discovered that we could not get up, and laughed even harder when we had to crawl over to the wall to climb up. We limped off the court still laughing at ourselves. When we stepped outside the enclosed room, two men were near the door waiting for their scheduled time on the court. The men were stretching and flexing, something my friend and I had neglected during our warm up.

"You guys done already?" One of them asked.

"Yeah, the people before us got done early and we were able to use their time and ours," my friend fibbed.

"We were the people before you," the other man said looking slightly confused.

"We like to get in two hours of play, but someone, I guess it was you," he said snickering, "Got our other time slot. We took a break after playing and came back."

My friend and I looked at each other, burst into another round of laughter, and then limped out of the gym.

The next day, I ached in places I had forgotten I had. Years before, when I had played racquetball, I would also ache, but I was young and still able to push past the pain and was just dumb enough to go back for more. I didn't foresee the impact that rigorous exercise would have on my body in the years to come.

Our culture encourages exercise and activities that are rigorous and competitive. It demands that we push beyond our natural abilities and limitations in order to win at something we don't do otherwise. Think about the number of people you know who suffer from major injuries that happened while playing sports that have nothing to do with their jobs, sustaining their families, or building a better community.

When I look at the exercise habits of people in

other cultures, I see an amazingly simple commonality: people exercise daily, with regularity, slowly and evenly. Most often, the people exercise the same way their entire lives and are able to do in old age what they did in their youth. They don't jog or play football. Instead, they walk or ride their bike to the park, where they join up with the members of their community to discuss life, exercise (often *tai chi* or *chi gong)* or take a light stroll. In some countries, neighbors meet weekly to dance to folk music, sharing news from the week's events. These community gatherings help sustain the physical and emotional well-being of the participants.

We Americans like to exercise like a line from the Ike and Tina Turner version of "Proud Mary:"

We never, ever, do nothing nice and easy...
We like to take things fast and rough."

You would think my venture into racquetball taught me a lesson: *stop it with all the family fun fitness.* But where exercise was concerned, my learning curve was flat. I decided that what I needed was a bigger group; something that could take the pressure off just a few people and spread it out over many. I mentioned my need for group fun to my manager Jeanine and she put together a kickball tournament. She sent out an invitation to about twenty people with the expectation that not everyone would want to attend.

To our delight, everyone wanted to get in on the activity, and they told others. We were astonished when 75 people showed up at my house ready to play kickball on the front lawn. The friends Jeanine originally invited said that when they mentioned it to their friends, everyone was excited. Most folks hadn't played the game since they were in elementary school, and everyone had memories of running and playing until their parents called them home. The average age of the participants that day was somewhere around 40, and that's only because my children and the few other young folks who showed up brought it down.

We trash-talked each other about who was going to whip whom. While people arrived, I decided to warm up my game. I stretched a bit and asked my son to pitch a few balls so I could get my kick in gear. The first few kicks went great, and I was feeling my oats. I pointed towards my neighbor's house, indicating that I planned to kick the ball over our half-acre lawn, across the street, past a home with an even bigger yard and into the pond behind the house. My son, who is extremely shy, laughed out loud and pitched the ball to me.

I reared back to get all the momentum I would need and connected with the ball even better than I had hoped. The ball soared and I forgot that the kick was just a warm up kick. I took off running at full speed. Now, in case you've forgotten, I was big; at that point I was well over 250 pounds. I heard something snap, but cars were still pulling up and people were watching me. I ran all the bases, and by the time I made it to home plate, my foot was as big as the ball that I had sent all the way over to the neighbors' backyard, missing the pond by just a few feet. I fell over in real agony, but my friends and the people they brought with them figured that I was joking, so they laughed and congratulated me on my big kick. When I showed them my big foot, they encouraged me to walk it off.

"I got Bertice," someone yelled, picking me for their team. Though the pain was getting worse by the minute, I beamed with pride. I thought back to my fat childhood when I was hardly ever picked for any sporting activity. I was usually the last pick, chosen just before a boy we called Pee Pee, because .... Well, you can figure it out.

On the day of the kickball tournament, I was chosen first. I ignored the pain and swelling in my foot and limped over to the illustrious place of "first pick." When it was my turn to kick, I must've been experiencing what athletes call "the zone," because after just a short while, I no longer felt the pain. Now that I think about it, I couldn't feel anything from my waist down. I limped to home plate to the sound of cheering from my team and trash-talk from the other.

"Yeah, Bertice. Send it back across the street," a teammate said. "You got this!"

"Get back," someone from the other team yelled. "She kicks high, but she can't run."

The ball came at me in slow motion. As I reflect on that day, I think I may have even heard the sound of grass bending and folding as the ball rolled over it.

I pulled my leg back and kicked as hard as I possibly could, but this time when I connected with the ball everyone heard the sound of bones and tendons giving way to old age, lack of use and being "broke down." I fell over in so much pain that I couldn't think or see straight. My sons helped me off the field in what television sports announcers called, "the agony of defeat." I sat on the sidelines and watched as my team was defeated 35 to 2.

Now, common sense would tell you that I went to the doctor after the game was over. But if my mother were still alive, she would tell you that common sense ain't common. Instead of having the foot x-rayed, I put on a bigger shoe and went back to my hectic lecture and travel schedule. I waited an entire week before I went to an emergency room to find that I had broken my foot, two toes and had torn muscles and tendons in my leg. This injury was only the beginning of a series of falls and sprains that would follow. I soon learned that when a part of the body is damaged or off balance, it opens up the possibility for more damage if it is not cared for.

I continued to travel and work through the pain, but the pain medication made my head cloudy. Speaking on different topics for completely different groups each day required that I be lucid, so painkillers were out. I never drank alcohol so I couldn't even "drown my sorrows" at the end of the day.

I did as most hard-working people do, I kept on working hard. **Too often, we ignore our body when it cries out for rest, proper exercise or food.** I have also been guilty of ignoring my needs and emotions while taking care of those of everyone else. When I tried to do something about it, I rushed headlong into exercise, as if rushing could ever be equated with being well.

Where exercise was concerned, I have learned to do the opposite of what Ike and Tina said to do in "Proud Mary." I now take it nice and easy.

In later chapters, you will learn how to create a plan for movement that fits your lifestyle and level of activity while yielding optimum results.

What exercise activity did you attempt to do only to find that it would not work?

Describe an event where your ego exceeded
your physical ability.

What activities do you do regularly with friends and family?

What event would you like to organize?
Describe the ideal activity.

Have you ever been injured while "having fun?"
Describe a time when you were sick or injured, but you
"pushed through."What would you
do differently?

Notes

"When you walk with Purpose,
you collide with Destiny"

CHAPTER FOUR

It's Just Stress

Nobody knows the troubles I've seen.

Nobody knows my sorrow.

—*Negro Spiritual*

NOTHING IS MORE STRESSFUL TO THE BODY THAN stress itself. In the 1930's, scientists recognized stress as the inability of a body to respond appropriately to emotional or physical threats. When a person is stressed, or even perceives themselves to be, there is a measurable change in their physical wellbeing often resulting in an elevated heart rate, headaches, and an inability to think clearly or to react appropriately. Stress has been linked to heart disease, disease of the immune system; including cancer, high blood pressure, and more.

Stress also causes weight gain. I believe that

stress adds more weight than overeating, but we rarely make the connection.

When I started gaining more weight than normal, I assumed that I was stressed as a result of the weight gain. It didn't occur to me that it could be the other way around. Stress also causes weight loss, which was the case for me after the death of my sister Myrna.

There is a saying that has appeared on tee shirts and bumper stickers:

I'm too blessed to be stressed.

This saying stresses me. Too often, hard working women and men ignore the signs of stress and its related illnesses because they don't want to appear weak or out of control. Any life change can cause stress, even the good ones. I know that I am stressed because I'm blessed.

The three most stressful events in life have been cited as the death of a loved one, divorce, and a major move. I experienced all three within a year. But in our culture, we hide behind an *appearance* of wellbeing. We drive big cars up to a big house that's has a huge closet full of clothes for covering a body that is sick from within. We proclaim that we are blessed and favored, while others around us are lacking and without.

Because I grew up in extreme poverty and have experienced a great deal of success, I have also carried a tremendous amount of guilt for having "made it." Many of my friends and colleagues who have similar lives feel the same. They express a sense of responsibility to those who have been less fortunate and are struggling to find their way. It's often hard to relax at home or on a vacation when close relatives can't pay their rent or utility bills. I vacillate back and forth between feelings of restraint and a sense of responsibility. I argue with myself for being "too generous," to those who should have made better life choices, only to give in to my overwhelming need to help. I recognize that my generous nature has helped me to get to where I am; it is truly more blessed to give than to receive. But I have come to see that **those who care a lot, carry a lot.**

We carry the stress and all of its physical manifestations for those we care for. The stress of caring for my mother, children and at times family and friends, has had a tremendous impact on my wellbeing. My choices to do more for others than for myself, led me to a place of illness, but as my brother/friend Marlon Smith pointed out, my misery has become my ministry. My illness led me to find a path to wellness that has helped many others.

I believe that the way out of the misery is back through it. By looking back over my life, habits and behaviors, I have been able to discover, or better yet, uncover information and wisdom that has been around for centuries, but is just now being fully understood. Nothing in the Year to Wellness program is new. What makes it different is the way the elements are combined and applied.

The first step was to see myself as a whole person, beautifully and wonderfully made. By doing so, I was able to find whole body solutions which yielded results that were beautiful and wonderful.

Do you see yourself as stressed? Make a list of three stressful events that happened today.

How has stress affected your health?

What do you do to alleviate stress?

List three stress releasing techniques you use.
How often do you apply them?

Notes

"When you walk with Purpose,
you collide with Destiny"

Chapter Five

A Little Child Shall Lead Them

It's a lot easier to heal the body than
it is to heal the mind.
—*Pediatrician, Dr. Steven Hobby*

LIFE IS A WONDERFUL AND BEAUTIFUL THING. As my mother used to say, "If you live long enough, you get to see everything come right back around."

When my daughter Fatima was diagnosed as "obese" I realized that I had been looking at weight all wrong. My daughter's diagnosis was the *coming back around* that my mother had talked about; this time though, I was able to see life more clearly. I have my daughter's pediatrician to thank for that.

When my family first moved to Georgia, I asked friends and health care professionals for the name of a good pediatrician. My three youngest children ranged in ages from 10 to 13 and I needed to find a physician who could see them all on the same day, as scheduling around their school and activities was cumbersome.

Dr. Steven Hobby came highly recommended. When we met him, I knew that we had found not only a good and thorough physician, but I could also tell that he cared a great deal about the children he served. He spoke to them honestly and encouraged them to ask questions about their health and lives. He took the time to listen to each one of them, and he always asked about their future plans.

The oldest two children, Jabril and Mariah, were long and lean and had almost "perfect" height-weight ratios. But the youngest, Fatima, was short and stout. Before we met Dr. Hobby, Fatima had been told by other health care professionals that she would have to watch her weight because as they said, she was just "too fat." One nurse actually asked her if she wanted to get married someday. When Fatima nodded her little head, the nurse said "Well, you'll have to lose some weight."

At this point, I spoke up. "Are you married?" I

asked the nurse. "Yes, I am." she said smiling. I turned to my daughter and hugged her.

"Don't worry, baby girl." I told her. "Somebody married her. You're not nearly as big as she is, and you are much nicer." We left that doctor's office and never went back.

Doctor Hobby had a completely different approach to childhood adiposity. After performing routine screenings and checking the children's blood work, Dr. Hobby came in to the exam room smiling. "You are a very healthy girl," he said to Fatima.

Fatima smiled her big happy grin and proudly said, "I try to eat all of the good stuff." Doctor Hobby then asked if he could examine the back of her neck. She allowed him to do so, and he explained that he was looking for an indicator of genetic adiposity.

"Just as I thought," he said. He asked Fatima if it was okay if I looked too, but I was already walking over to look. When I did, I saw the small dark bumps that encircled the back of her neck. Dr. Hobby said that it was "cutis ansernia" or goose flesh. He told us that this was an indicator that Fatima was genetically predisposed to being fat. Fatima's eyes got wide, and she had the look she got whenever she made a connection to something bigger.

"Then what is this?" She asked, pulling down the side of her pants exposing stretch marks that I had not seen before. Dr. Hobby said, "Yes, this is another indicator and it tells me that you are growing faster than normal." Fatima looked as if she had just won her spelling bee; something she did regularly.

I explained to Dr. Hobby that I was concerned about her weight. I told him that I did not want her to have all of the weight issues I had experienced, and that I wanted her to be healthy. Dr. Hobby turned to Fatima and spoke directly to her while I wondered who was paying the bill. He said that she had to try hard to maintain her weight but not to try to lose any.

I thought I'd heard incorrectly. "What do I need to do?" I implored.

"Do nothing." He said plainly. He continued saying, "I don't want you or Fatima to become obsessed with her weight; it will only add more." Dr. Hobby said, looking directly at me.

"It's a lot easier to heal the body then it is to heal the mind," he told me. **"When the mind is messed**

up, it's almost impossible to heal the body."

I was astonished. This was good science.

Dr. Hobby went on to say that if her weight remained the same, then over time she would get taller, average out, and be just fine. But if I obsessed about it, she would too, and the dieting would cause her to gain more weight than she lost.

Turning back to Fatima, Dr. Hobby said, "When I see you next year, I want you to weigh exactly what you do this year." Fatima was all smiles. She had been given permission to be herself, something I had been afraid to do.

It's been five years and Fatima weighs the same as she did when she first went to see Dr. Hobby. Every year, he tells her how impressed he is with her progress. She's a bit taller and very shapely and she loves herself and her body.

Dr. Hobby's approach was the catalyst I needed for looking at weight differently.

The public is just beginning to see the science on genetic factors in fat. Every day we hear about differences in metabolism, cortisol levels, insulin factors and thyroid research that all point to different causes of weight loss and gain. Still, too often physicians take the easy route and suggest pills, surgeries and diet plans that don't address the real, underlying issues, have short term impact, and, worst of all, dangerous side effects.

My daughter's diagnosis as obese and the treatment by her pediatrician became my gestalt; the eye-opening experience I needed to find my own way to wellness. I started to look at weight gain as the result of factors other than overeating and lack of exercise, but finding a physician who would confirm this proved to be very difficult.

Most of them followed the same script we all do, that weight gain causes illness, not the other way around.

Even when doctors see weight differences as genetically predisposed, they still view it as a genetic defect. This view leads to a cycle of dieting, weight loss and then weight gain—a pattern that I had become all too familiar with.

One day I was suffering from severe joint pain that was a result of arthritis. In the past, my physicians had told me the pain I suffered was a result of the weight I carried. "Lose weight and you will be fine," they all told me. The pain had become virtually unbearable, so on the recommendation of a friend I went to see a naturopath. Mark Armstrong, or Dr. Mark, as he is often called, is a licensed naturopath in Atlanta, Georgia. He stands about 6 feet 5 inches tall and is a soft spoken man with a calming demeanor. Dr. Mark asked questions about my life, family relationships, my work and how I lived life from day to day. He spent a great deal of time listening and coaxing me to describe situations and conditions with great detail. Before he made any conclusions or prognosis, he asked me what *I* thought might be going on with me. At first, I was thinking, "Hey, you're the Doctor, or whatever it is that you are."

But I decided to give the method a chance. Doctor Mark not only pointed out the connection between the mind and body; he also spent time talking about the spirit.

I have always been a spiritual person. I have often felt that the only thing that has kept me going was my spirit. I mentioned this to Dr. Mark and he agreed, but he reminded me that my spirit lived in a body, and therefore it was my job to care for the body that housed my spirit.

After several visits to Dr. Mark that included treatments of acupuncture, energy realignment, and allergy testing, I was able to look at wellness from a more holistic perspective. I began to read and study information and ideas from other cultures and belief systems. I put these ideas into practice and immediately began to see results. As I did, others asked for advice, so I began to share with them. By doing so, I was able to fine-tune a program that became my Year to Wellness plan. As a result, I have erased the health problems and illnesses and have lost 150 pounds. Others who have been on this journey have reported weight loss, wellness, and most of all a sense of wellbeing that included better relationships to others and to themselves.

When Dr. Mark first saw my results, he asked for advice for himself and his patients. He also encouraged me to share the plan with others.

In the following pages, I will outline my plan and then help you become a co-creator in your own Year to Wellness.

Have your experiences with your physicians been positive? How have they viewed the relationship between health and weight?

Have you ever tried alternative medicine?
Describe the treatment and the outcomes.

If you have children, how do they feel about their weight? If you don't know, ask them.

As you prepare yourself mentally for change,
what do you think you may need to do?

Notes

"When you walk with Purpose,
you collide with Destiny"

Here I'm singing with members of the International Spa Association. You are beautiful, you are wonderful, you are powerful; just as you are, just as you are.

I am smiling in every picture. Be happy at every stage and remember, you can't get the body you'd love until you love the body you have.

Right: When I was in High School, one of my teachers told me that I had "Such a pretty face." He said that if I lost weight, I could be beautiful—I was and am beautiful and so are you.

Bottom left: Before and after; The Year To Wellness Plan will enable you to lose weight while becoming fit and tone. Prepare yourself for drastic change.

Dance now. Enjoy the energy and life you have at any size. Change will come. Enjoy the journey.

Celebrating 50 and playing dress up. 50 is the new 50!

Section II:

Change

TERMS OF AGREEMENT

IF YOU'RE READING THIS, YOU ALREADY HAVE WILL power, discipline, and the ability to sacrifice things you enjoy to reach a goal. Chances are you've already been on at least 5 serious diets. You are most likely tired of the gimmicks, foods and fasts that accompany the get slim quick exercise and diet plans. We all know that Wellness is not easy, so I'll be up front with you:

This is not a diet.

It is a wellness plan that requires a change of attitude, habits and ideas that you have about yourself and your body.

Wellness will not happen overnight.

The Year to Wellness plan takes a year. You will not be slim in six days, six weeks or in six months. An entire year of small changes will provide you and your body with the opportunity to gradually adapt to and maintain healthy habits for living.

The program is progressive.

You really cannot do step five before you
have completed step one. Like it or not, knowledge
is cumulative. You can't do college algebra
without a basic understanding of multiplication.

Assume you don't know.

Most of what you think you know about wellness
was taught to you by an industry that makes 56 billion dollars a year by keeping you uniformed about
true wellness. Be as diligent about letting go of old
ideas as you were in adapting to plans
that did not work.

Listen to your body.

You've listened to doctors, lawyers and Indian
chiefs (Okay we haven't really listened to the Indian
Chiefs; if we did, there would be more of them to
listen to). Now you will learn that the body, specifically your body, is an amazing machine designed to
repair itself. When we are in tune with what it can
do and why its' turned against you, you will be in a
position to learn what your specific needs are.

There is nothing new under the sun.

The newness lies in the way we combine and integrate old wisdom with new knowledge.

Do not skip the first section.

While it may be tempting to want to jump right into the program. It is crucial to understand the "why" behind how you got here in the first place.

Read this book first and then begin your wellness plan. Do all of the reflection exercises at the end of each chapter before moving on to the next.

If you have read and understand this agreement, please sign and date this

Wellness Agreement Form:

Name_____

Date_____

Introduction to Section Two

True Wellness

We have more degrees but less sense; more knowl-edge but less judgment; more experts, yet more prob-lems; we have more gadgets but less satisfaction; more medicine, yet less wellness.
—Theologian, Bob Moorehead

THIS SECTION WILL OUTLINE A WELLNESS PROGRAM that can be incorporated into an everyday lifestyle for being healthy and whole. The Year to Wellness Program starts by enabling you to reassess the way you see yourself so that you can approach your wellness goals from a perspective that is not one of self-loathing.

While most weight loss programs assume that fat is a result of overeating, research indicates the opposite; that poor self-image, hormonal imbalance and improper nutrition and hydration lead to weight gain. **A healthy plan requires that people actually eat more frequent but smaller meals of the foods they need rather than fewer calories of the foods they believe they want. Our approach requires healthy eating throughout the day.**

Additionally, proper exercise or "moving" will be defined and encouraged as a tool for a healthy lifestyle. Most exercise gurus have never been fat and do not understand the physical constraints of a larger person. More importantly though, their programs use a high impact approach that often results in injury and can actually lead to metabolic disease.

The Wellness program in this book will also discuss stress reducing techniques as a means for weight loss, including massage, meditation, visualization and sleep therapy.

The information in this healthy approach is not new. Some of the tips are based on ancient practices while others are grounded in the latest scientific research. What makes this program unique is that it operates under new assumptions—fat is not always caused by overeating.

Additionally, a poor self-image and weight discrimination adds weight. It must also be stated that I
do not equate fat with unhealthy or unattractive. **You
can be beautiful and healthy at any size.**

This plan will assist you in setting goals and getting results that are defined by you, not by the fashion
industry, the media or insurance companies. This approach is not an attempt to add one more diet to the
pile of bad programs. It outlines a plan for *embracing
and loving you* as you are creating while maintaining
a holistic approach to a healthy lifestyle.

**True wellness, is the alignment of the spirit/en-
ergy of a person with their mind and body.** It is not
just the absence of disease as some allopathic physicians argue, nor is it only the state of feeling well and
balanced as some naturopathic practitioners believe.
Wellness is a state of Being, wherein an individual
is whole and complete, and their spirit/energy, mind
and body exists in a harmonious, balanced state.

**The only person you can change is <u>you,</u> so let the
change begin.**

Chapter Six

A Year to Wellness: The Plan

A Change is gonna come.
—*Singer, songwriter, Sam Cooke*

By now you should know that this plan requires commitment for at least one year. Beyond the cost of this book, there are no hidden fees, fine print or renewal charges. You will not be required to join any gym or facility, and there will be no monthly meal plan automatically shipped to your door. The real and most important cost will be your decision to finally take care of you.

I have observed that those who care a lot carry a lot. We carry the stress, strain and often the weight of those we care for. But when all of our attention is given to those we serve, leaving nothing to ourselves, our own health falls into decline and illness. Look down the hallways and into any "break" rooms of your nearest health care facility. You will see that many of the health care providers are not healthy themselves. These are people who have to leave their lunches mid-bite, and run to emergencies that for them have become routine. Without adequate nutrition they grab the high calorie snacks, sweets and fried fast foods that overfeed but under nourish. Caregivers are a lot like the hairdresser who never has the time to style her own hair but has a reputation for being the best stylist in town.

Decide today that you deserve the time that this program will require. Dedicate yourself to reclaiming your health and fitness with a commitment to you.

Cleaning the Filter

I think that every life has its own filter. It's similar to the filter in a front-loading clothes dryer with a note that reads, "Clean before each use." The filter on your life is there to collect your negative past experiences, but it needs to be routinely cleaned; otherwise the past experiences become the window through which you see the world. If you've had a bad relationship but don't let go of the pain, you will view the next relationship with suspicion and mistrust waiting for the same bad things to happen again and again.

I should know. When I got divorced after less than a year of marriage, I wrote a country song called, *If I Shot You When I Met You, I'd Be Out of Jail by Now.*

Put your guilt and shame about the past in a bag with all your old diet pills, thigh blasters and plastic sweat suits. (I'd tell you to throw them out but none of those things are biodegradable.) Guilt and shame have never been good motivators and most often lead to self-loathing and often depression. Recognize that you have a year to adjust to change. If things don't go perfect one day, **decide to be better the next.**

With much gratitude and a renewed perspective, let your wellness begin.

Phase One: Mental Cleanse

The first three days of the program are the most difficult. They require that you change the way you see yourself.

During the first three days of your program, begin each morning by identifying what you like about yourself. Be as detailed as possible. As the day progresses, give your body gratitude for carrying you around. (By now you may want to throw this book at me, but before you do take another look at my "then and now" pictures and think again.) Changing the body requires changing the mind.

Cellular regeneration of the body's organs happens every 11 months. Every ninety days, we renew our blood, and it takes two years to change our brain cells. We cannot effectively change our body unless we change the matter that the body has available to do the work. When you feed your body inadequate fuel, hydration and thinking, it will be weak and not capable of operating at its optimum best.

Cellular development is contingent upon fresh oxygen, water nutrients, exercise, rest, relaxation and recreation (Staib 2010). In order for you to truly change your habits you *must* also change your thinking about yourself.

During the day, reflect on your past diet trials and errors. Replay moments and incidents of abuse and discrimination. This is the hardest part of the Wellness Plan. Reliving painful events is, well, painful. Try to play these events back without judgment towards your own self or the others involved. As the events unfold in your mind, project forgiveness onto those who have mistreated you and healing for yourself. You may choose to journal your observations or simply talk to yourself in the mirror.

After I had success with my own Wellness Plan, others asked me to guide them on their journey. They would call regularly to share their observations, struggles and successes.

Sally, a woman in her forties who had previously tried numerous diets, reported that while on this phase of her Year to Wellness plan, she talked to herself daily, telling herself that she was beautiful and deserved to be well. She noted that she not only felt better, but also looked better to herself and to family members. "I can't describe this feeling," Sally said. "I'm just so clear. My skin is clearer, and so is my thinking."

Brenda, a 58-year-old, highly educated professional, tried to begin the plan without going through the three day mental cleanse. She felt that weight loss had more to do with what she actually gave up, not what she thought or believed about herself. She lost weight at first, but then went back to old eating habits and feelings of low self-esteem.

Brenda started the plan again, this time including the three day mental cleanse phase. She reported that this time her weight loss was much more rapid and that she was able to maintain her progress. Brenda has not only lost weight, she is in better health and has better relationships. She said that for the first time in her life, she is learning to really love herself.

While Sally talked herself through the three day period, Brenda and others kept a written log of their experiences. Those who journal reported that that they often woke up at night from dreams of old repressed memories and felt compelled to write them down. At the end of three days, they would reflect on the things they had written.

Let's Begin: Remembering

Think of the time when you first felt fat, ugly, lazy, unattractive, of all the "lovely" things we tell ourselves. Think of why you felt this way. What were the events surrounding your experiences? Replay the events in your mind.

Your memory can play tricks on you. Sometimes, we see things the way we "feel" they've occurred. Over time, we add and delete details to justify our beliefs concerning the other people involved, the time of the event, and even the event itself.

According to neuroscientist and Alzheimer researcher Richard Mosh, memory does not exist as a thing you can touch; it is a concept that refers to the process of remembering. He points out that memory is not located in a particular place in the brain, but is a brain-wide activity. Your memory, he points out, is made up of a group of systems that all play a different role in creating, storing and recalling memories. When the brain processes information, all the body's systems work together to create a cohesive thought. (Mohrs, *How Stuff Works,* 2010).

Some homeopathic practitioners and healers believe that every part of our body reacts, learns, and remembers. They argue that our bodies hold memories of both pain and joy. Whether the memories are true or fabricated, they will still have an effect on our physical body.

Remembering correctly is critical to the process of establishing new ideas and patterns of behavior. Old, inaccurate thoughts are what led you to the feeling of dissatisfaction in the first place.

Look at the pictures from a period where you thought you were fat. Try to remember the events or ideas that gave you those impressions. Once you remember, allow yourself to be forgiven. Forgive yourself for not seeing your beauty, and let it go.

Some participants created ceremonies of forgiveness. Such ceremonies can be as simple as lighting a candle, or saying a meditation, prayer, or affirmation. The more involved you are with the process, the more impact you will have on your outcome. You are also creating new habits, new memories and new ideas for yourself. The more senses you involve in the activity, the more heightened the memory around it will be. This will be helpful for replacing old habits with new, healthy ones.

Forgive Others

During this process, you will undoubtedly recall events when others have said and done harmful things to you. If you are to move forward, you <u>must</u> forgive these people as well.

Forgiveness is not about letting someone else off the hook, it's about getting off the hook you've been put on. **Forgiving others is for your own benefit.** It does not require that you go to and individual and announce that he or she is forgiven, nor does it mean that you have to let this person back into your life. It simply and beautifully allows you to let go of your hurt and shame and to forgo any need for retribution or punishment. You can create small ceremonies of forgiveness like saying a prayer of gratitude, lighting a candle or releasing a balloon. I have often written letters forgiving others and myself. I then tear up that letter or burn it in a fireplace. I may even make up a happy song about letting go as the paper burns.

As simple as those acts are, they trigger and help create new memories for healthy habits.

Gratitude

The roman philosopher Cicero pointed out that gratitude is not only one of the great virtues, it is the parent of all others. The law of attraction states that what we think about, we bring about; in other words, what you give energy to, will expand. By showing gratitude to yourself and to the body you have now, you will be able to attract the wellness you desire.

Start each day by thanking yourself for breathing, moving and desiring to be better. Send a message to your entire body that you are grateful for all that it has done.

Sit comfortably and relax. Breathe in and out deeply and calmly. Starting with the top of your heard, acknowledge your entire body. Thank your head, neck, shoulders, arms and back. Continue throughout your entire body being as detailed as you desire. Continue to breathe deeply and allow yourself to relax. Thank every part of your being. As you do, you will begin to smile from within. Your gratitude is like a charge to a dead battery. You are giving yourself the energy you need and deserve to go on through another day. Breathe deeply and enjoy the feeling of renewal.

Three Days Is Not Enough

The three day mental cleanse is a way to kick-start

your thinking by helping you recall how you got to where you are in the first place. A three day physical cleanse cannot erase years of bad eating, nor can a three day mental cleanse erase years of bad thinking. It is a start. You will find the need to redo this exercise throughout your Year to Wellness. End each day with a statement, thought or prayer of gratitude for what you have been able to accomplish and an acknowledgment of love and forgiveness for the areas where you may have fallen short.

Recognize this beautiful truth: **"Where there is breath, there is life and where there is life there is hope."**

How did your thinking and processing
of old memories change your eating?

Did you eat more or less during this time
of recalling and reflecting?

Do you see any changes in how
you look and feel?

Have others commented about your appearance?

Do you feel more peaceful, calm and relaxed?

Has your sleeping changed?

Do you have more or less energy?

What other observations have you made?

Notes

"When you walk with Purpose,
you collide with Destiny"

Chapter Seven

Waking Up the Metabolism

"Do you know how to establish, regulate and direct the metabolism of your body; the assimilation of food stuff so that it builds muscles, bones and flesh? No, you do not know how consciously, but there is a wisdom within you that does know how."

New thought author and speaker, Donald Curtis

YOUR METABOLISM IS THE PROCESS BY WHICH food is turned into energy at the cellular level. When the metabolism is slowed down, food is not easily converted into energy and is therefore stored as fat. This can be the result of a genetically predisposed metabolic syndrome, or as a result of not eating enough of the right kinds of foods. We often hear about empty calorie foods; foods that are high in processed sugars that contain little or no nutritional value. Empty calories are difficult to convert to energy and are stored as fat.

Too often, metabolic disease goes undetected and so is not treated. Because of weight bias, doctors often fail to diagnose thyroid conditions or even diabetes in their fat patients.

It is remarkable that Oprah Winfrey, one of the world's wealthiest people, suffered from a thyroid condition that went undetected for years. Physicians often believe that weight causes our problems, but they fail to detect the illnesses that are causing the increase in weight.

One day I saw one of my neighbors in the grocery store. She commented on my weight loss, and I noticed that she had lost weight too. I told her that she was looking wonderful and she said, "Well I've only lost 30 pounds."

I am still surprised when people place the word "only" in front of any weight loss. I told her that this was tremendous progress and that I was happy for her, knowing that she had been struggling with her weight and self-esteem. I asked her if she was taking a healthy approach and she laughed.

My neighbor told me that for years she had complained to her doctor about being tired and sluggish but that he would always tell her that she needed to lose weight. She got tired of his response and went to a new physician. She shared the same symptoms with her new doctor and the doctor ordered a series of routine tests. My neighbor soon learned that she was diabetic and was prescribed the necessary insulin regulating medicine. Within a week she was feeling better and immediately started to lose weight. Since that day, I have seen her walking or riding her bike around the neighborhood. She says that she now has the energy to exercise and feels good enough to get outdoors again. Fat people must demand the proper health screenings that other people automatically get.

Before you begin this or any wellness program, get the necessary screenings and checkups from your physician or naturopath. Ask for a metabolic screening (required for newborns, but not adults) to determine if you are genetically predisposed to weight gain. Even if you are, don't worry, you will be able to boost your metabolism and increase wellness. Knowing what your health issues are is the first step toward changing them.

Eating All Day Everyday

I first learned how to eat at Red Mountain Spa in St. George, Utah. I had been invited to speak there after hosting the national conference for the International Spa Association. I've been asked to come back to the conference year after year to inspire the people who own and run the spa industry. The audience is always full of some of the most physically beautiful people I have ever seen gathered in one place, and I came to learn that they were also beautiful people in spirit. The folks at ISPA never made me feel self-conscious about my weight. In fact, they made me feel beautiful. Members would stop me in the hallway of the convention center to tell me how wonderful I was and how beautiful I always looked. One year, someone yelled out in the audience of about 3,000 people, "I love you Bertice, you're beautiful."

Every year I looked forward to being with the folks at ISPA. With them, I learned many of the lessons I used for my own wellness.

At Red Mountain Spa, the cuisine was very healthy, but also extremely tasty. The executive chef, Dale Van Sky, explained to me that by adding natural seasonings he could reduce or eliminate the use of the more fattening ingredients, but maintain the flavor, while helping the body to heal itself. "The food is good, and it's good for you," he said.

I asked why it was so filling, and he told me.

"Empty calories leave you feeling empty, but real food gives you what you need."

One afternoon at the spa, I heard a few guest lecturers speak on nutrition. The husband and wife team of a nutritionist and licensed dietician, Drs. Chris and Kara Mohr, had helped LL Cool J develop his famous abdominal muscles and had been advisors to other celebrities as well. The Mohrs pointed out the fact that American portions are much too large and encourage overeating. They shared their seven fat busting strategies (www.Mohrresults.com) and I incorporated some of them into my Wellness Plan. I started by using the smaller nine inch plate and by eating with smaller utensils. The Mohrs' suggested that by doing this, you are less likely to shovel in large portions of food without having the chance for it to be chewed and digested properly. The process of digestion starts with the first bite. When you are chewing, you are already digesting your food. By chewing food more, you are helping the digestion process before the food even gets to your stomach. Some nutritionists recommend that you chew each bite 20 times before swallowing it.

This is helpful information. While you may not be able to do this each time, you will find that by being aware of how fast you chew and swallow, you will be more active in your own digestion.

Your brain needs about 20 minutes to get the "I'm full" message from your stomach. By eating more slowly and chewing more, the brain has the chance to get the message that you are full before it is too late to stop eating. The Mohrs also recommend that you try eating with your less dominant hand. This helps balance your coordination and slows down your eating.

Six Beats Three

Smaller meals more often allow you to get the right amount of food more regularly. I eat six times a day instead of the recommended three meals. This allows me to keep my metabolism running like a fine-tuned machine. It also helps to stay in front of my hunger. Take a moment and think about the eating habits of the thin people you know. Chances are, you can picture them constantly chewing. Naturally thin people eat more often, but they eat smaller amounts when they do. This "grazing" reduces the sluggishness you feel at the end of a large meal and provides you with the right amount of food that can be converted to the energy you need.

Mary reported that before she started the program, she would get home from work tired and hungry. She often grabbed the high carbohydrate, starchy foods we ironically call "comfort foods." But by eating smaller, more frequent meals, Mary was able to reduce her desire for the fast foods she had made a habit of.

Caring For You

Caregivers, health professionals and people who manage the lives of others tend to skip meals throughout the day. They are so busy taking care of others, that they have no time to care for themselves. These people often appear to be overeaters, but they are more likely to be undernourished eaters; finding filler foods such as candy bars, other high sugar fixes, energy drinks, coffee and sodas to curb the appetite and give quick bursts of energy. Additionally, caring people also shoulder the stress of others. The additional stress causes even more weight gain.

Preparation Versus Willpower

Willpower only works some of the time. Fat people typically have more willpower than our thinner counterparts. Every day, we must will ourselves to go through a world of weight bias and our own self-hatred. Even when diets fail us, we will ourselves to come back for more. If willpower alone was enough, we'd have been well long ago. **Preparation is better than willpower.**

Michael Jordan is one of the best basketball players who has ever lived. His fans often debate whether his greatness comes from his learned brilliance, or a natural physical ability to fly high and score big. According to Michael Jordan himself, what makes him great is his preparation. Jordan always arrived at least one hour before his teammates and opponents to every practice and ballgame. Michael said that he utilized the quiet practice time to focus and to prepare himself for the task of winning.

I've learned to approach my wellness the same way. I had to be prepared for delayed flights and crowded runways. I stopped asking flight attendants for extra cookies and snacks, because I pack my own healthy foods. Prior to doing this, cookies were sometimes the only thing I would eat all day while traveling. Sometimes, I forgot to eat altogether.

Like many fat people, I often skipped breakfast, finding it difficult to eat early in the morning. Most days, I would eat my first meal around 11:30am or after noon. Nutritionists constantly remind us that breakfast is the most important meal of the day, as it actually *breaks* the bodies *fast* from the night before; hence, break- fast.

Dieticians say that you need to eat within an hour of waking up, thereby allowing your digestive system and metabolism to awaken as well. This is common sense, but remember sometimes common sense is just not that common.

For many Americans, the first meal consists of coffee or some other caffeinated beverage and a donut, muffin or pastry. The caffeine dehydrates the body while the sweet breads make us hungry.

Try starting the day with a protein shake or small bowl of oatmeal, without all of the sugar, butter and milk. (Try raisins as a sugar substitute.) As a vegetarian, I like to start my day with a vegetable juice or a small salad.

All behavior is learned and anything that is learned can be relearned. **We have grown accustomed to our bad habits, but we can also substitute them for good ones.** When you dedicate yourself to small changes in your eating habits, the body will respond favorably, allowing yourself to begin to heal.

Reflections and Exercises

Every morning pack or prepare the foods that you will need during the day. When food is already prepared it is easier to grab and eat. This is time consuming but so is television, internet surfing, and gossip. You deserve to be well, make time for you.

Set an eating alarm on your computer, hand held device or alarm clock. If eating smaller healthier meals more frequently is not a habit, you will need to be reminded to do it. Once you are accustomed to eating frequent healthy meals, you will no longer need the reminder.

Keep a journal of what and when you eat. This can be a note on the back of a napkin or in an actual food journal. The easier it is to journal, the more likely you are to continue. When you become more mindful of what and when you eat, you will be capable of determining which foods work best for your body.

Purchase a water bottle/cup and drink water after every meal.

Make time to go to the bathroom. As you eat and hydrate your body more regularly, you will need to eliminate waste more frequently. Be prepared to go as often as necessary. Holding it is not a healthy habit.

Is eating throughout the day difficult?
Is it tedious? Why?

How are you feeling?

How are you looking to yourself and others?

How are you sleeping?

Notes

"When you walk with Purpose,
you collide with Destiny"

Chapter Eight

Food Is Making Me Sick

"Food is an important part of a balanced diet…if
you are going to America, bring your own food."
Author, Fran Lebowitz

HI, MY NAME IS BERTICE BERRY AND I'M A POPCORN-aholic. I've been overdosing on popcorn since the night I was stood up for my senior prom and I discovered the soothing effects of salty, sweet, crunchy combination.

I'm a popcorn gourmet. Popcorn makers like Dale and Thomas, Garrett's in Chicago, and Nuts on Clark, couldn't stand up to a popcorn challenge with me. Sometimes I mixed my popcorn with combinations of nutritional yeast with nuts and raisins. For the more daring, I combine hot popcorn with home-made caramel, I then drop in cut up pieces of Snicker-Bars. The result, surprisingly, is not too sweet with a hint of salty.

Needless to say, I've had a long-time love affair with nothing but popcorn. It turns out though, I am allergic to corn.

When I discovered this "minor" detail, I knew that something was not right in my world. What would normally have been a small snack of one bowl (cooked, not micro-waved) would cause abdominal cramping, bloating and indigestion. I ignored all these symptoms and looked for other reasons for my body's sudden rejection of popcorn.

What my body was saying loud and clear was, "I've had enough." Too much of a good thing is not a good thing at all.

We all have a food or beverage that we love so much we can't go through the day without it. For some people it's diet soda, for others it's packs of chewing gum. The item can be obvious—like macaroni and cheese—or not so obvious, like peanut butter. These foods tend to be related to some emotional event whereby it serves as a reminder of the comfort you've felt by eating it.

The problem is, these foods can also be allergens or *trigger foods*, empty calorie foods that serve as a trigger or gateway to eating even more. When I ate popcorn, I couldn't get the nutrients my body needed. Adding cheese does not count, so even after finishing off an entire bowl, I was still hungry and improperly nourished. I'd go from popcorn to something else, trying to get what I needed. But as I've said before, empty calories are empty calories.

Once you have started eating healthy, you will be ready to figure out one of the most important ingredients to becoming well: what you should <u>not</u> eat.

After introducing your body to eating more small meals every day, pay close attention to the way you feel, think, and look. Which foods give you gas, which leave you feeling hungry or anxious? Which foods make you nauseous and which give you short bursts of energy followed by sluggishness?

<u>Your</u> body will inform you which foods are easily digested and which ones are not. Listen closely to what <u>your</u> body tells you and you will gradually be able to create the plan that is specific to your true needs.

We are all different, unique individuals. What affects your health may not be a problem to someone else.

The beauty of this plan is that it allows you to co-create a program that is specific to your individual needs. Once you determine your "popcorn" or trigger food, begin to create habits of avoidance. This will be somewhat difficult at first. You may need to wean yourself slowly or you may find the cold turkey method most effective.

When Mary first began to listen to her body, she soon learned that diet sodas were making her bloated and anxious. Mary started each morning with a jumbo sized diet cola. Why not, there were no calories, right? But what the diet soda lacked in calories, it more than made up for in acid, artificial sugars (which the body does not distinguish from real sugar) and gas. Mary had a very difficult time even thinking about giving up diet cola.

"I need my soda in the mornings," she said. I asked her how she could possibly "need" soda. I asked which vitamin, mineral, or protein it provided.

Mary said, "Well, none, but it wakes me up."

I pointed out that she was already up and driving by the time she purchased her soda, so the wake up thing was not working. I asked if the diet cola was high in Omega 3's and she said, "Stop. I see your point, but I *need* my diet soda."

I asked Mary to think about her love affair with diet soda and to come back with the real story.

Later that day, Mary called and got right to the point. "Okay, here's the real deal. You can drink all the diet soda you want and it doesn't have any calories. It's the one thing I can have large servings of, but not feel guilty about." She went on to say that when she was growing up she was not allowed to have diet soda or much regular soda at all. One of the first things she did when she was on her own was to buy all the diet soda she wanted.

We all have those "when-I'm-grown-I'm-going-to-get" foods (I have a thing for Lucky Charms). Sometimes we allow our childhood wishes to drive our adult choices, but the results are still childish.

I know adults who munch on sugary cereals, potato chips or cake for dinner because they couldn't do it when they were young or simply because they like it. Like it or not, we need to grow up and away from the emotional choices we make regarding food.

I told Mary that her body was starving for real breakfast. Mary would go until midday before she had a meal. By then, she was starving for nutrition but instead, she grabbed fast foods that were filling and quick. Most days though, she would just drink diet soda until she was on her way home from work. Then she would make a mad dash into the fastest fast food place in sight.

You must eat breakfast. You must let go of the emotional food that is making you sick and replace it with healthy choices of vegetables, proteins, fruits and whole grains. Smaller servings more frequently will enable you to tune into your body's needs.

Letting Go

Where the mind goes, the body will follow. Research shows that a successful diet or wellness program must include an emotional component as well. (Cleland, et, al, 2002). In other words, if you want to effectively change your eating, you must change your mind first.

Everyone has a definitive moment when they decide "enough is enough." Dieters, though, have this definitive moment over and over again. There were two events that stood out for me. One was the inauguration of President Barack Obama. As I watched the inauguration on TV with millions of others, I held my last bowl of popcorn and cried.

In his address, the president pointed out that America had a lot of work to do on its economy, health care reform, and a host of other issues. The president said that he knew that the American people were up to that task. He pointed out that the government had to do its part, but that individuals must do theirs as well.

I had accomplished much in my life. I had climbed up from poverty, earned a PhD, was raising my five adopted children and volunteering in all kinds of community outreach programs. But there was more that I could do. I decided right then, that if the president was going to work with congress and the senate to bring about healthcare reform, then I was going to work to be healthy. I savored each kernel of corn and decided then that I no longer needed it. Whenever the urge or craving for popcorn came up; which by the way has been every day since, I tell myself **"I already know what it tastes like. I like the way a healthy body feels better."** At that time of the inauguration, I didn't know what running a 5K felt like, I didn't know what wearing a size six felt like, and I didn't know how it would feel to go into a doctor's office without worrying about what they would find. As I watched the inauguration, I made a choice to change forever.

The other event happened a month later when my nephew Christopher died of a massive stroke brought on by undiagnosed hypertension. His death forced me to remain committed to my goal to be well.

When friends would try to tempt me with popcorn, I'd smile and say, "No thank you, I've had enough." And I have. I'd been eating it every day since I was seventeen. I had had enough. I decided if I never had it again, I'd already had more than my share.

What Inspires You?

Find the thing that motivates you to change. It can be the birth of a grandchild or the desire to sit in a movie theater chair. **When we are inspired by some-thing, we are less likely to feel as if we have given something else up.**

One day, I was in the Chicago airport, the home of Garrett's Popcorn. If you've never had Garrett's Gourmet's popcorn, don't. I travel a great deal for work, so I have learned which airports have which specialty foods.

Prior to this day, I almost always had to leave my flight terminal in search of Garrett's. This time though, my flight was boarding right next to the shop. There is an old proverb that says we attract what we fear, love, and desire. I love and desired popcorn and I feared that I would not be able to give it up. So as far as that proverb goes, I was three for three. I fought with myself on whether or not I should just have just one more bag for old times' sake. I told myself that I was doing great and that I knew what popcorn tasted like. Then my weakness rose up and said, "But when will you be back in Chicago? You can't get this every day." I told myself that I could make any popcorn I chose to make and that I didn't need it.

I kept talking to myself, but was walking towards

the popcorn shop anyway. Just as I got up to the line—there is always a line—a gorgeous man came from seemingly nowhere and walked right up to me.

"You are a fine sister," he said.

"Thank you," I beamed. "And I'm going to stay that way, too."

The man must have thought that I was crazy, when I practically ran away from him and the popcorn shop. I felt as if God, fate, the angels, and all that was good was on my side in that moment, and I know that they still are. But the simple fact is that I had a choice: popcorn or wellness. I chose wellness.

We all need a push to do the right thing. That day, mine came in the form of tall, dark, and handsome. Still, I could have chosen to think that since he thought I looked good, I deserved a reward: popcorn. The real and lasting reward, though, was to continue on the path to wellness that I had started out on.

Too often when we are successful in getting well, we reward ourselves with the same treats that made us unhealthy in the first place. Imagine an alcoholic celebrating his sobriety with a drink or a lung cancer survivor celebrating remission with a pack of cigarettes. **When you "treat" yourself with the foods and beverages you are trying to eliminate, you wake up the old desires to have them again and again.** When I am successful with a new healthy behavior, I reward myself with another healthy behavior, and I encourage you to do the same.

After two weeks of healthy eating, reward yourself with a massage or facial. The money you've saved from lattes and fast food binges will be more than enough to afford a massage, facial or other healthy gift. Luxuriate in the fact that you are becoming the healthy person you were always meant to be. **A trigger food is not a "little taste," it is the gateway back to the behavior you are now trying to change.** Close the door; you already know what it tastes like.

Over time, your urges will become weaker and weaker, and you will begin to crave the foods and beverages that promote wellness. Your body already knows it needs them; you are simply learning to listen to what is mentally, emotionally, and physically good for you.

What food(s) or beverages do you think
that you cannot do without?

How often do you have this food or beverage?

What are its nutritional values?

What is the emotional value? In other words, how does this food or beverage make you feel and why?

Can you remember when you first started eating this?
How did it make you feel?

Go a day without this food or beverage
and make a note of the following:
How do you feel?

How difficult was it to give up?

When you started to crave the food,
what did you do instead?

Try again tomorrow and answer the questions
again.

Which nutritional foods do you enjoy most?
Look for recipes that include those favorable ingredients
and experiment with new ways to prepare your meals.

Make a list of the healthy rewards you would like
to have (massages, facials, a day of rest).
Make a reward plan for when and how to earn them.
(After a week of wellness, I will take
a trip to the park.)

Notes

"When you walk with Purpose,
you collide with Destiny"

Chapter Nine

Cut It Out

*"God gives every bird its food, but He does not
throw it into its nest."*
—*Novelist, J. G. Holland*

WHEN WE THINK OF A DIET OR EATING PLAN, ONE
of the first things that come to mind is deprivation.
"I have to give up bread and butter for the next six
weeks", or "I won't get to eat any sweets." **True wellness is about the healthy habits you take on, not the
things you give up.** By eating a small meal every two
to three hours, you will reduce, and then eliminate
the desire for what I call *filler* foods; the foods we
grab to fill us up after we have been starved of the
nutrients we need. Smaller, more frequent meals will
also reduce your dependence on pick-me-ups like
caffeine and energy boosters.

So what can you eat? Most Americans have grown accustomed to diet plans that tell them exactly what to eat for each meal. I am bombarded with inquiries about **exactly** what to eat. "What's in your bag today?" interviewers will ask.

My mother had a wonderful saying, "What I eat won't make you go to the bathroom." (She used more colorful words, though.)

The foods that work for my body's needs and the daily activities I do may not be right for you. As I've said, I am a vegetarian. I initially became vegetarian for weight loss when I was thirteen, but over the years I have been more intentional about my vegan diet. What I eat won't make you move.

Every dieter knows the caloric counts, grams of fat from sugar, even the amount of carbohydrates in their foods and beverages. **We have become a nation of fat calorie counters, so obviously counting calories doesn't work.**

Determine what you like, but try new things. Our palates are amazingly boring. We eat the same meals weekly rarely trying new things. (It's Tuesday. We have hot dogs and baked beans on Tuesday.) Remember, this is <u>your</u> year so even if you are preparing food for others, take the time to prepare special meals for yourself. When you become well, others will want to do the same.

Add fresh herbs and new seasonings. Try new ingredients and see what tastes good. I recently had cilantro on fresh fruit. The spicy-sweet combination was something I would not have thought of before but it was amazing. **There is no one diet plan for everyone.** We are unique in every way. Unfortunately, we have not spent enough time experimenting with foods that we truly like and that are compatible with our bodies. We eat what we have eaten for most of our lives. We rarely try anything new.

Food preferences vary by region, race, and ethnicity—and to some degree by religion. Our food choices are as segregated as our lifestyle. The more open you are to new ideas, cultures, music, art, and thinking, the more likely you are to vary your food choices. I know all too well what popcorn tastes like, but there was a wide range of vegetables, I had never ever tried.

We make choices based on what's in front of us, what our parents taught us and what we have become accustomed to. Open your mind and mouth to new foods.

When you are planning your daily meals, try something new weekly to see if you and your body like it. The greater the variety, the more likely you are to keep eating, fueling your body with healthy choices and therefore avoiding the empty calorie, filler foods.

There are some things you will need to give up. We've already discussed the need to let go of the negative thoughts you have about yourself. You will also need to give up the following things.

Appetite Suppressants

Appetite suppressants work against your body's needs. You are not fat because you are greedy. You are fat because your metabolism is not regulating properly and your body is storing fat rather than turning it into new cells, tissues and muscle. When you suppress your appetite, you are not allowing your body to tell you that it needs to be fueled. You don't need to skip meals, you must eat them. Your meal may be a handful of nuts or an apple, but you need to eat. The very best way to suppress a desire to eat junk is by eating something nutritious.

Anti-Gas Pills

We've all seen the advertisements for the pills that you take before you eat something that you already know will give you gas. You may have even tried them. If you become gaseous after certain foods, you may have to eat them a different way (cooked versus raw or vice versa). You may need to add natural herbs to the cooking process (parsley or sage), or you may have to eliminate these foods from your diet completely.

When you alter the digestion enzymes your body produces naturally, you are causing damage.

Likewise, if you have to regularly pop antacids or chase a meal with carbonated beverages, you are eating something your system does not digest well.

The over-the-counter pills and antacid medications block the signals that report the malfunction. It's like taking the batteries out of the smoke alarm because it annoys you when it goes off. You need the alarm to tell you when something is on fire. It is also necessary to allow your body's alarms to report to you that foods are not agreeing with your system.

Girdles, Tight Clothes and Shoes, Oh My!

Let's be frank, body slimmers are not making you slimmer. They are cutting off the flow of energy throughout your body. Tight clothes and shoes do not make you look more stylish, thinner or more beautiful; they make you look uncomfortable.

Naturopath Mark White teaches that **what hurts the body will not heal the body.** When you squeeze into things that are too small, too tight, and uncomfortable, you are doing damage to your circulation, metabolism, and your natural ability to breathe. Moreover, fat smoothed out in one place will only ooze out of another.

Processed Foods and Artificial Sweeteners

Recently, there are lots of reports on the negative effects of processed foods in your diet. These effects include damage to metabolic rate, respiratory disease, and heart failure. Processed foods and artificial sweeteners are believed to affect asthmatic conditions, promote ADHD, cause skin disorders and even promote cancer. (The George Mateljan Foundation, 2006)

The field of research on preservatives, trans-fats, sulfates artificial colors, and pesticides found in processed foods is extensive and somewhat cloudy. However, all of the findings indicate a rather critical point: that the body treats the additives in processed foods as a disease or poison. Your antibodies attack these alien objects the way they would any alien presence that seeks to destroy you. This would be like repeatedly calling in a SWAT team to get a cat down from a tree. After the second call the team would not respond, even if the cat was joined by a hungry lion. When the team is truly needed the energy and resources will have been misdirected.

Processed foods do not give the body what it needs. Real foods that grow from the ground or come from animals that actually walk around on it are better for you.

Barry, a man who began the Wellness program recently, had a difficult time giving up potato chips. He tried everything but still struggled with his love of chips. Barry is a good cook, so I suggested that he make his own chips from sweet potatoes, beets, carrots or other veggies in a light olive or vegetable oil. He did and was astonished to find that he was full after eating just a handful.

I do not know all of the ingredients that are in processed foods. I can't even pronounce the ingredients listed on the labels, but I'm almost certain that some of those chemicals are designed to make you want more of those foods. By eating real foods, you will get the nourishment your body needs to regenerate cells.

Dr. Howard Murad, a leading dermatologist and founder of the Inclusive Health Center in California, points out that **Americans are overfed, but undernourished** (Murad, 2009). We eat larger quantities of artificial products, growth hormones and beverages laced with artificial sweeteners and stimulants and are left fat, agitated, hungry, and damaged.

The rapid rise in weight gain is directly correlated with the increase of preservatives in our foods. We often compare ourselves to the people in other countries and wonder why *we* are so fat.

On a recent trip to Korea, I noticed the one

cultural difference that stood out above the politeness, respect for elders, and quiet beauty: the huge amounts of foods South Koreans ate.

Before I could complete one course, another was being served. I asked a Korean friend why everyone ate so much and where they were putting it. She explained that the huge meals were cultural, that because South Koreans had survived war and famine, they made sure that they were never hungry. As a vegan, it was hard for me to find food. Meat or fish was in almost every dish. Rice was served with most meals and there were also desserts, usually pastries and fruit. While Koreans tend to walk more than Americans, the main difference in weight may be accounted for by the limited quantities of processed foods they consume. Every meal was prepared from real food ingredients.

Begin to reduce the amounts of prepackaged and processed foods in your diet. You will find that you are fuller, have more energy, clearer skin, healthier hair and nails, and your digestive system will become much better regulated.

Comparison

Curiosity did not kill the cat, comparison did. When you compare yourself to others, you will always come up short. There will always be someone who is thinner, better looking and richer. But remember, no one can be *you*. Find your unique qualities and celebrate them now.

We have come to think that the diet that works for others will work for us also. We also expect to lose weight at the same rate as others. Our bodies are as unique as our minds. If you try to lose weight too fast for *your* body, you run the risk of causing damage to your metabolism and becoming sick as a result.

This is a good time to discuss The Set Point Theory and weight replacement.

Developed by William Bennett, MD and Joel Gurin, the theory points out that our bodies are biologically and genetically predisposed to maintain a specific weight range and level of body fat. (Bennett and Gurin, 1982) The research argues that we have no control over our body's weight range, which is why after reaching a certain weight we have a hard time losing additional pounds. If, through crash diets and pills we do accomplish weight loss, the weight will come back, or it will be as I call it, ___replaced.___

Dieters often experience uncontrollable urges to binge. Bennett and Gurin believe that this is the body's way of telling you that you need more food to function properly. Too little food will result in a slow metabolism because the body wants to hold on to what it has.

My set point is different from yours. Too often though, we compare the number on the scale to that of some starving Hollywood star. When your body has reached its ideal weight, or set point, you will find it difficult to lose or even gain weight. For now, it is important to understand the need for letting go of comparison.

"I am fearfully and wonderfully made."
—Psalms 139:14

The Need To Constantly Weigh Yourself
Weighing yourself is a necessary aspect of weight loss. (Duh!) However, weighing yourself constantly can be a distraction or worse, discouraging. Our

weight fluctuates greatly within a day, a week, or a month with no changes in eating behavior. These fluctuations may be the result of the time of the day, the amount of stress we are under, and for menstruating women, their monthly cycle.

When you start your wellness plan, weigh yourself once a week at the same time of day. The seven day cycle will give you a more accurate read on your progress. Don't freak out about the rate of loss, or even temporary gain. This slight weight fluctuation may be a result of any number of factors. Fixating on the number on the scale will cause you to lose sight of the big picture. A healthy rate of weight loss is one pound per week. That's 52 pounds in one year. Research indicates that a slow rate of weight loss will enable you to keep the weight off permanently. You will also have less loose and sagging skin. My weight loss was greater than one pound a week. It all depends on the amount of weight you need to lose, but a steady pace will result in a much healthier you.

Naysayers

Most likely you have encountered friends and family members who are negative about healthy living. These people are everywhere. Misery doesn't just love company, it loves miserable company. Those who are not happy with their own weight and health issues will be negative about the changes you are making. When possible avoid and disengage from these negative people. But sometimes it's not easy to separate ourselves from family members, co-workers, bosses, fellow church members, neighbors, and friends.

As the saying goes, you can run but you can't hide. When loved ones, friends and colleagues berate, ignore and belittle the changes you are making, erase the impact with the understanding that they are only doing what they know, and that if they could do better they would. Resist the need to argue or defend the changes you are making toward a healthier you.

As you become well, your friends and family can learn from you. But until you fully learn and adopt a healthy lifestyle, remain quiet, calm and steadfast.

What filler foods do you need to eliminate? List them.
What can you replace them with?
Make a list of the healthy foods you would like to try.

Find and create recipes that include healthy ingredients. Write out one day of healthy eating. Prepare it for tomorrow.

De-clutter your pantry. Look for the foods that are past their expiration date, have been in your cupboards for more than six months and anything you want to avoid. Remove them.

De-clutter your closet. Pick a day and go through your closet and eliminate all but two items that do not fit. (Those two can be incentives.) Donate the other items to friends or charities. (Note: Sometimes they are the same.) Also remove shoes and girdle-like garments that pinch and rub.

Weigh yourself three times in one day and note the fluctuations.

Who are your naysayers? Make a list (in your head for safety) of the naysayers in your life. How do they affect and influence you? How do you affect and influence them? (This is often a two-way street.)

Outline ways to ignore or eliminate the negativity.

Who do you compare yourself to? How do you compare yourself to others? Why do you compare yourself?

Reward yourself and celebrate your changes.

Notes

"When you walk with Purpose,
you collide with Destiny"

Chapter Ten

Start Moving

"Energy and persistence conquer all things."
—*Ben Franklin*

THE NEXT TIME YOU ARE WATCHING A TELEVISION program and you see one of those infomercials for a weight loss program that does not require exercise, turn the channel.

When you meet a personal trainer who tells you that you have to do strenuous boot camp-like exercises to lose weight, walk slowly in the other direction. But when you find a DVD, class or activity you absolutely love, make it a part of your daily habits.

Exercise or movement as I often call it is an integral part of a healthy lifestyle. It helps to reduce stress, maintain your weight by regulating your metabolism, heart rate and blood pressure. Proper exercise promotes a positive outlook on life by increasing endorphins and boosting our level of energy. The right exercise helps align the back and body by strengthening your core or abdominal muscles and it promotes healthy aging, increasing life expectancy. (Mayo Clinic, 2009)

The issue is not whether we should engage in exercise, the real issue is the type, length and frequency with which we should engage. It's essential to find the exercise program that's right for you.

Learning new habits require that we focus on the first things first. With the Year to Wellness Program, you will not begin a movement routine at the same time you are starting your new eating regimen. You could not learn basic math and algebra at the same time.

One reason people drop out of weight loss programs is that they try to do too much too soon. Give yourself six to eight weeks of healthy eating before you begin your movement and exercise program.

People will continue to do what they enjoy, find convenient and excel in. Starting a Wellness plan with a high level workout that requires an already fit body is just not a good idea.

Before doing any exercise program, consult with your physician or naturopath and make sure that your program will not be harmful to your health. Start out gradually by doing energy flow exercises like Tai Chi or a slow paced stretching program. If you have done little or no exercise, you will need to gradually reintroduce yourself to moving. Even water aerobics may be too strenuous for the true beginner. There is no shame in being a newbie, but there will be a pain if you try to do too much, too soon.

When I first started on my Wellness journey, I tried to do the same exercises I had done when I was in my twenties. I went back to heavy weight lifting and attempting my five mile run. (I can hear you laughing.) I quickly learned that I was out of condition, old and broke down (and that's the technical term.) At first I enjoyed the challenge and told myself "no pain, no gain." But I tired easily and began to crave popcorn again. I switched to a stretching and toning routine that I continue even now. The result was an injury free effective workout.

I am often asked how I lost weight so quickly

yet don't have any sagging skin. I believe that one of the reasons I'm tone and fit is because of the weight loss exercises that helped my skin maintain its' elasticity. This was a gradual process. When I first started, bending and stretching was accompanied by a symphony of cracking sounds. As my body regained its agility, my joints were able to move with ease. I avoided exercise fads and flashy packaging and stuck to the old school calisthenics type routines (Jack LaLanne is in his 90's and he is still doing the same old exercises.)

Dancing is another healthy way to get your body moving. Start with five to ten minutes of dancing to music you love. Make sure you start with a warm up song first (The Flashdance song, "She's a Maniac" by Michael Sembello is not a good choice.)

Gradually increase the length of time up to, but not exceeding thirty minutes. I have found that like eating, smaller amounts of exercise more frequently have a greater impact on weight loss.

My favorite exercise is walking. You may like to ride your bike or swim. While I enjoy them all, walking works with my lifestyle. I don't need a gym, or perfect weather. On rainy days, I walk inside my home with a DVD walking program and sometimes I walk around the living room.

Because I travel a great deal, and often get to my hotel after dark, I am not likely to exercise outdoors or go to the hotel gym. Instead, I work out in my room.

What works for you? A good program is one that you can do now, can increase or decrease in intensity over time, and is a routine that you enjoy and will continue. Too often though, we choose exercise programs the way we choose diet plans; based on the promise of unrealistic results and marketing mumbo jumbo. The right exercise for your body should not be selected based on how it worked on someone else's body. Remember, we are all very unique.

As you become more comfortable with your routine, increase your intensity and the number of times you exercise each day.

I exercise six days a week, and rest on the seventh. **The body needs a resting time for recuperation and muscle repair.** Use your day of rest for relaxation, massage and for learning more about wellness.

Every week you will find new ways to become a healthier you. As you become more fit, identify group activities that you can do with your family. My children and I enjoy badminton (Okay, maybe I'm the only one enjoying it, but they humor me and play along,) swimming, bike rides and hikes. The more enjoyment you get from the activity, the more likely you will be to do it over and over again.

Exercising regularly will require a commitment from you, so remember, **we do not commit to what we don't like.** Just as you have changed your thinking about the foods you eat, start to renew your mind concerning exercise and movement. You <u>must</u> move to be well, but you must find a form of exercise you like. We must renew our way of thinking about exercise and physical activity by starting with movements we can do and will continue, and most of all, enjoy.

What physical activities do you most enjoy?
Is this activity practical for your everyday life?

Create a ten minute exercise routine that can be done in your living room, bedroom or office.
Keep a log of your activity. (Write it down in your Wellness journal). Be mindful of your activity.

As a reward to yourself, purchase a pedometer or other type of body movement meter and log your activity. (They range in price from 5 to 50 dollars.) I never leave home without my pedometer. By measuring steps I am reminded to keep stepping.

How have your energy, outlook and appearance
changed since your program started?

Notes

**"When you walk with Purpose,
you collide with Destiny"**

Chapter Eleven

Beautiful You

"Beauty is eternity gazing at itself in a mirror."
—*Poet, Kahlil Gibran*

ONCE YOU BEGIN YOUR JOURNEY TOWARDS WELLness —the harmony between the spirit, mind and body— you will become more beautiful physically, emotionally and mentally. In addition to the intentional healthy eating and movement programs you co-create, you will need to incorporate the following practices and treatments into your lifestyle.

Hydration Therapy

A healthy body is a hydrated body. Our bodies are sixty to seventy percent water. We need water to regulate our body's temperature, to get oxygen to our cells, to remove waste, to protect our joints and organs and to transport nutrients to your organs. (Jegteiv, 2007)

Only twenty percent of the water we need comes from our food. The rest comes from drinking good old H2O—not water infused with Crystal Light, Kool-Aid or tea. When you've added powdered drinks or tea, it's no longer water.

Nutritionists have found that the amount of water you need daily varies based on your weight, the amount of outdoor activity you do and the amount of caffeine you have. (The more caffeine, the more water you need.) To determine the amount of water you require, divide your weight in half. This is the **basic** amount of ounces you will require. (e.g., 140 lbs—70 ounces of water)

Practically every soda company now sells bottled water. As we have become more health conscience, water has become more readily available. You can purchase it from the same vending machines that carry sodas and energy drinks. We carry water bottles and cups more than ever before; and this is the problem. While we may be *carrying* more water around we are not drinking it.

Try to drink water in the morning when you first get up and start moving around. Do this before breakfast, even before you brush your teeth. I drink at least two glasses of water before I start my day. Hydrating the body is beneficial to your skin and promotes a more beautiful you. Drink a full glass of water after every meal. It helps with digestion and weight loss.

Water is also necessary for the outside of the body. I've always been overly sensitive to hygiene. As a big person, I was prone to sweat more and was therefore more attentive to my body's oders. When there is a bad odor and a big person in the same room, the big person is usually blamed. When I was a child and teased about my weight, the subject of hygiene almost always came up. I took special care with cleanliness and have maintained this habit even now. When I started to live my Wellness plan, I got into the habit of taking long hot baths.

I had spent so many years bathing, caring for and grooming the hair of my children, that at night I had little time left for myself. I'd stumble into a quick shower and then fall into bed but was still unable to sleep. A hot bath after a long day relaxes the body and enables you to rest more fully.

Massage

I've mentioned earlier that massage is critical to your wellness plan. Before I started on the wellness journey, I suffered from painful arthritis and the pain of old injuries that had not healed properly. Additionally, I suffered from poor circulation. The extensive amount of business travel I did only added more pain to my ailing back, knees and joints.

I searched for the right massage therapist, and found one. Together we created a massage program that helps to promote weight loss. Massage reduces stress and helps regulates cortisol, the stress hormone. When cortisol is too high or too low, we are more likely to store body fat. Therapeutic massage also helps promote muscle building.

I recently interviewed six-time Tour de France winner Lance Armstrong, who said that when he is training and before and after every event, he gets a massage. Lance said that massage helps with endurance, performance, and stamina. (ISPA Conference 2009)

Massage also helps to increase tissue metabolism and improves your muscle's range of motion and flexibility and is believed to be able to directly aid in fat reduction. Massage helps heal the body but also helps to heal the emotions.

Proper touch can help heal the wounds of improper touch. When I volunteered at a nursing home, teaching wellness principals to the staff there, I hired a massage therapist to work on the overworked, overstressed and underpaid staff once a month. At first, it was difficult to get the employees to try something different, but after they saw the effects on co-workers, everyone was in line. After receiving a brief chair massage, most of the women would cry tears of relief. Many had never experienced massage and some reported that they had never really known proper touch.

Including massage as a part of my wellness program has made a tremendous difference for me. I've noticed that when I skipped a weekly massage, I didn't sleep as well, and my body had more aches and pains.

In the past few years, massage has become much

more available and affordable than ever before. Massage therapists are setting up chairs and tables in malls and airports. They make office visits and will come to your home. However, all massage is not equal. Find a Board Certified therapist near you. Before making an appointment, place a call to discuss your needs. Let the therapist know that you are fat and ask if they have any other large clients. Listen closely to determine if they would be comfortable, knowledgeable, and experienced. Like anyone else, the massage therapist may have also been socialized to be less sensitive to the needs of a big person. I have found, however, that a good massage therapist is especially attentive to every client's needs, regardless of weight or size.

When you find a good therapist, work with them. Schedule appointments and keep them. Let them know all the areas of pain or any issues of concern.

Once you have established the working relationship and schedule, try to work out a financial arrangement that is comfortable for both of you; a regular client is always a bonus. Also let your therapist know that you are willing to tell others about their services. Finding the right massage therapist is essential, when you find of one who works well, let others know too.

Folks on a budget may try calling a massage school to find students who need hours of practice to get certified. They may provide the service free or at a very reduced cost.

Sleep and Relaxation

The athletic exercise equipment manufacturer, Nautilus, now manufactures mattresses. The Nautilus Sleep System was created to give athletes the best sleep for relaxation and muscle recovery. The Nautilus researchers recognized that if they were going to make the best exercise equipment, they would need to match it with the best sleep system.

The body needs rest to recuperate, regenerate, and to renew. Your mind requires rest for downloading and processing all the data from the previous hours. We all know that we need eight hours of sound sleep every night. For some reason though, we make excuses for not getting the thing our bodies needs most: rest. We would never think of trying to drive a car without refueling, changing the oil, or getting a tune up. You know this is not wise, yet this is what you do to your own body when you "overheat" it by not getting the rest you need. Getting a good night's sleep aids in weight loss which will not occur without it.

For years I slept only four to six hours a day. I burned the candle at both ends and when those ends burned down, I burned the wick in the middle. But the body has a way of getting back at you for all the damage you've done. The things we get away with in our youth will catch up to us as we get older. I'm certain that my weight gain and the illnesses I suffered were related to my lack of sleep. I'm not sure if the chicken or the egg came first, but what I do know is this; as I learned to sleep better, I began to feel better.

There are many websites developed to provide you with information for getting a good night's sleep. There are also books, programs, and therapies. Before you take any over the counter drug or prescribed sleep aid, try to engage more natural methods for rest and relaxation.

I have created rituals and habits for sleeping more soundly. I have gone from sleeping a few hours, waking up for two and sleeping for two more, to deeply sleeping an entire eight hours.

Here are my recommendations:

Turn off the TV

Television affects your rest, food consumption and mood. Turn it off at least two hours before sleeping for a more restful night. If possible, remove the TV from your bedroom completely.

Take a bath at night

Take a hot bath with essential oils like lavender or chamomile for a more restful sleep.

Have a cup of tea

Lavender and chamomile teas help to promote rest. The warm beverage is also soothing.

Oils, lotions and soaps. Use essential oils, lotions and soap on the body and try them in linen sprays or a drop of oil on your pillow. Lavender is a wonderfully relaxing ingredient for a restful night's sleep.

"Don't let the sun go down on your anger"

Try to go to bed with a light heart. Avoid arguments, gossip, and disciplining your children before going to bed. Everything looks more positive after a good night's sleep.

Read and be grateful

Use the time before bed to read a good book, journal
or mentally remind yourself of all you have to
be grateful for. Gratitude helps to eradicate fear
and also reminds us of how far we've come.

Rest Well.

Skin Exfoliating and Moisturizing

Every day, a thin layer of dead skin cells accumulates
on the surface of your body. When you are shedding
pounds, you must also shed your own skin. Exfoliating is the removal of the outer layer of dead skin
to revive the newer layer. It unclogs pores, helps reduce breakouts and keeps the skin clear. Additionally, exfoliating the body allows you to give attention
to areas that have been ignored. I exfoliate my skin
at least four times a week and am always amazed at
how in the past I had given little attention to elbows,
the backs of my knees and my huge thighs. Using
gentle scrubs and buffs on the skin will give it a more
youthful glow.

Moisturizing is also important for more beautiful skin. Lotions, creams and oils are more affordable and should be used daily. The more you massage, exfoliate and moisturize your body, the more you assist it in weight reduction and maintenance.

By now, you may be wondering when you will have time to do all of this. In later chapters, we will outline ways to slowly introduce new habits into your wellness plan. For now, it is important that you remember that you deserve to take time for yourself. **As you reward yourself with healthy habits, you will have less and less time for unhealthy ones.**

Visualization

To become more beautiful, you need to perceive yourself that way. **Creative visualization is the practice of affecting the physical world by changing your mental thoughts.**

Pioneers of the New Thought Movement of the 19th century like *Science of the Mind* author Ernest Holmes and the author of *The Science of Getting Rich*, William Walter, believed that creative visualization was one of the main tools for reaching a goal.

Visualization techniques are used by the world's

top athletes for becoming the best in their sport. These athletes practice mentally seeing or visualizing their desired outcome over and over again, creating detailed images of their desired outcomes.

For weight loss and wellness, practice seeing yourself well. Instead of posting or hanging old pictures of yourself, create new ideas of how you should look at the age you are now. Mentally see yourself healthy, and imagine what it would feel like.

When I started my Wellness plan, I imagined myself with a body I never had. In my mind's eye, my legs were longer and more toned than ever. My arms were not big and flabby (as they were) but muscular and defined. My skin was healthy and youthful, and my stomach was flat. I borrowed the bodies of Venus and Serena Williams, the butt of one and the shoulders of the other. As unbelievable as this may sound, I have now become what I imagined myself to be. When I look back at old pictures I laugh and cry at my audacity. I wonder how, at 290 pounds, I was capable of believing in myself enough to get where I am today.

At 50, I look and feel better than I did at 30. As

corny as this may sound, I had to *see* it before I could *be* it.

Beauty is not only skin deep, it comes from the inside, and works its way out. As you are healing and reshaping your body, you will also need to constantly change your mind. Remind yourself to love every inch of you, as you are right now, and you will evolve into the version of yourself that you desire.

Are you drinking enough water?
Keep a log of the amount of water you drink.
How much do you consume? Make a plan
to drink even more water and execute it.
How did you do?

How do you sleep? Do you remember your dreams? (We all dream, we just don't always remember them.) How long do you sleep? Create a plan for sleeping better. (No, you can't get rid of the person next to you, remember, the only person you can change is you.)

Do you exfoliate and moisturize your
skin regularly? Purchase travel size products and try
them out. Use a skin glow treatment from a day spa as
a reward for staying the course. How did the treatment
make you feel?

What do you want to be when you grow up?
Create a visualization board, dream list and an idea of
how you want to look, feel and be.

Notes

"When you walk with Purpose,
you collide with Destiny"

Chapter Twelve

Hater's Gonna Hate

*"It demands great spiritual resilience not to hate the
hater whose foot is on your neck."*
—*James Baldwin*

I SET OUT TO UNDERSTAND WHY AS A STRICT VEGE-tarian who exercises every day, I had gained so much weight. The answer came to me in a beautiful and wonderfully weird way; the sewage system on my house kept backing up. (Stay with me, I already told you it was weird.) Week after week, the septic tank on my sewage system would be full and clogged. Fortunately for me and everyone else in my house, the system had an alarm and would ring loudly, letting us know that we were backed up. The city engineers would come out and drain the tank, change the motor on the grinder and, at one point, even changed the grinder. The problem happened over and over again. No matter what the workers did, in a week or less, we'd be back in the same situation.

At first I blamed my children, thinking that all the items pulled from the clogged system had been flushed by them. My children denied all the allegations as I expected they would. (What kid "fesses up" to an angry mother?) The children were steadfast in saying that they had not flushed down a dishcloth or a towel, and were not pouring grease down the drain, nor had they been using and flushing tampons. I could see that they were telling the truth, so I called the city's sanitation engineer to ask why my system kept backing up. The chief engineer explained that each house had an individual tank, and that all of the sewage that came from my house went there directly and then to a pipe on the main road. I asked if there was any way sewage from other houses could have gotten into my tank. He laughed and informed me that this would be impossible, since the back flow valve keeps anything from flowing back.

I said, "Well, that's it. The backflow valve must be broken."

He chuckled again and said, "You are not an engineer, so you don't understand."

I told him that he was correct, I was not an engineer, but a sociologist with a good understanding of statistics and probability and that the sewage in my system was probably not mine. He laughed yet again and said that he'd have the workers dig further to find the problem.

Later that day when I arrived back home, I found a note from the engineer. He apologized to me and informed me that they had somehow failed to put the back flow valve in, so I was getting all the sewage from all my neighbors—all forty houses.

Prior to my tank's repairs, my neighbors would stop by and ask why the city's sewage truck kept coming to my house. They'd shake their heads, smile and say things like, "Why I've *never* had a problem with my system."

The next day, after my tank had been repaired, my neighbors began to appear at my house again. They wondered what I had done to "mess up" their sewage systems. I informed them that I'd given them their "stuff" back.

After my back flow valve was repaired, I made a simple but wonderful observation; even though I'd done everything to keep my system clean, I was taking on the mess of others around me. This not only applied to my septic tank, this applied to my life as well. This is why I believe that those who care a lot also carry a lot.

I have always been inspired to do for others. Having grown up in poverty, I believe in helping others find their way. Still, too often I've taken on much more than I should, and have had to deal with the consequences.

When I decided to get well, I experienced a backlash from family and friends who felt that they were being ignored. When I refused to go out for lunch or dinner with friends I'd previously hung out with (and paid the bill for) I was accused of being standoffish. When my children would try to have "me time" during my exercise time and I told them to come back later, they'd stomp off and whine about my not caring. I turned down the numerous requests to volunteer for events, boards and other requests that affected the amount of time I had put aside for my own wellness. At first, I felt guilty for not "being there" for those who needed me. Soon I realized that if I did not take care of myself, I would not be able to take care of anyone else. I stayed focused on my wellness in spite of the obstacles, demands, and pleas of my family and friends.

My body responded rapidly to the changes I made. I dedicated myself to eating and moving more, and I was rewarded for the work. Still, I believe that the bulk of my weight (pun intended) was a result of the stress in my life. When I reduced the stress in my life, the weight followed suit.

In the first six months of my Wellness plan I dropped a whopping amount of weight (I'd tell you how much, but I don't want you to compare yourself to me.) Still, no one seemed to notice. My clothes were sagging and I was feeling great, but only a few people mentioned my weight loss. After eight months and another thirty pounds, no one recognized me. Even my dog Othello barked like he didn't know me. Old friends would pass me by on the street. When friends or old acquaintances arrived to pick me up from an airport, they'd drive right by.

"I wondered why that little girl was waving at me," My friend Mila said when she met me at the airport.

People began to ask what I had done to lose "so much" weight. When I tried to explain, most didn't believe me. They all expected to hear about a diet, a pill, or surgery. People began to whisper and gossip. Was Bertice ill? Did she have bariatric surgery? When I talked about eating small but frequent meals, getting massage, or my walking and toning routines, people often laughed. However, the more well I became, the less they laughed. Soon even my skinny friends were asking for help. From time to time I'd encounter people who, like me, had cared more for others than they did for themselves. When they desperately asked for help I gladly responded.

You don't really know if a plan is really valid until you can teach it to someone else. When your results can be duplicated, then you know that what you have is true and truly works. By helping others create their own Wellness plans, I have been able to see the power of my own Year to Wellness.

During your journey, you will undoubtedly encounter those who laugh, mock, or even attempt to sabotage your program. You will be offered more cookies, cakes, pies and chips than you have ever seen before. Candy will appear out of nowhere and hot dogs will hang from the trees. (Okay, I made up that last part, but you get the point.) Once you determine to be well, there will be those who try to deter you. Remember, if they could do better, they would.

When people are not doing what they need to do, they become bothered by those who are doing right for themselves. This behavior really has nothing to do with you. It is about the shortcomings the other person sees in themselves. You have become a mirror for what they know they should be doing.

Stay your course. Love yourself enough to get well and stay well.

Describe two periods in your life when you ignored your
own needs to care for others.
How did you feel about it?
What can you do better in the future?

Chances are, you have been on diets in the past/. Describe an event when you felt you were distracted, deterred or sabotaged. Write out a plan for avoiding the pitfalls you've experienced in the past. (Being proactive is extremely beneficial to continuing your program.)

Who would you like to share your Wellness plan with?
(Make a list, but for now, keep it to yourself.)

Notes

"When you walk with Purpose,
you collide with Destiny"

Chapter Thirteen

Co-Creator

"The creation of something new is not accomplished
by the intellect, but by the play instinct acting
from inner necessity."
—*Founder of Analytical Psychology, Carl Jung*

AFTER HAVING READ THE PREVIOUS CHAPTERS AND
completing the reflections and exercises in each, you
are now ready to co-create your own Year to Wellness Plan.

Week One: Gratitude and Forgiveness

Day 1: Start your day by forgiving yourself for not
loving you as you are.

Day 2: Begin to journal the events, diets and struggles that got you here. Remember to forgive
yourself for not being where you'd like to be and

for not loving yourself fully.

Day 3: Forgive those who have harmed you, and then let go of your pain. Remember forgiveness is for *you*. When you forgive, you are letting go of a need for retribution or the desire to see your offender punished. Let go and be free.

Days 4, 5, 6, 7: Write out your feelings and emotions from the first week, noting how you felt, ate, and slept. Spend time each day in forgiveness and gratitude.

Week Two: Start Eating

Day 1: Without any worries or concerns about what you are eating, prepare six small meals and eat every 2 to 3 hours. Make sure you drink a full glass of water after every meal. Start your day by eating within the first hour after waking up.

Day 2: Repeat the routine of the previous day, but eat with as much variety in food choices as possible. This will enable you to see what foods work well with your system and which do not.

Day 3: Continue to eat six small meals a day and make note of how you are feeling after each meal. (E.g.: Full, hungry, anxious, tired, weak, etc.) Adjust your portions and vary the food combinations and watch your results.

Day 4, 5, 6, 7: Continue eating six small meals a day *without* rigorous or regular exercise. Remember, your body needs to adjust to changes in diet before you introduce any changes in exercise.

Week Three: Finding Your Trigger

Day 1: Look back over the previous week and note which foods or beverages you felt you needed to have each and every day. Also note the foods you craved or grabbed when you were feeling stressed. Your trigger food is not as obvious as what you may have thought. It's not just what you really like, it's the food or beverage you feel you can't go without.

Day 2: Continue having your six small meals and water daily. Reduce or remove your trigger food. Remember, your trigger food may not be the same as mine. Remind yourself that the Wellness program lasts an entire year. You have time to gradually reduce the foods that you know you need to do without. By gradually removing trigger foods, you will not feel deprived. You will also notice that the more nutritional foods you eat, the fewer cravings you will have for empty calorie foods. In some cases, you may need to add something. Try having a tea instead of coffee, but add a boiled egg. Remember, *not* eating is *not* a way to get well. Additionally, high calorie beverages will only add to your cravings.

Day 3: Start your day with two full glasses of water 30 minutes before your first meal. Continue the day with your six meals. Make a note of your feelings. During this time, pick up a new book or hobby to replace the comfort food you removed.

Day 4: Hang in there. Repeat your hydration and eating as the day before and begin to note the changes in your appearance, feelings and attitude.

Day 5: If you haven't already done so, remove the trigger foods from your diet.

Day 6: De-clutter a space in your life: a desk, your closet, or even your Blackberry. What things did you find hard to let go of? What does this tell you about you? Eat as before.

Day 7: Pick a time in the day to weigh yourself and use this day as your regular weekly weigh-in day. How much weight have you lost? Remember your results will vary. The more steady the pace, the greater the likelihood that you will keep the weight off and remain well. Avoid the need to brag about your weight loss or get others to join you in your Wellness plan for now. Use your energy and excitement for your wellness and focus on yourself.

Week Four: Eating Better

Day 1: Create menus for six meals that are free from filler foods (breads, sweets, chips, etc.) Become more and more creative with your meals and learn to like new foods.

Day 2: Make a note of your overall attitude. Eat six meals and drink your water. Begin to cut out negative conversation (gossip, mindless chatter and negativity) and reflect back to the first week. Remind yourself that you deserve to be well.

Day 3: Replace the things you've removed with

healthy snacks. Research the best quick and nutritious snacks for your Wellness Plan. (For example: If nuts don't agree with you, don't eat them, find healthy snacks that do.) As you begin to truly listen to your body, you will discover more and more foods that should be eliminated. Listen and act. Keep eating and drinking your water.

Day 4: Begin to reward yourself for your progress. Instead of food rewards, give yourself something that will inspire and uplift. Reaffirm the fact that you are beautiful and wonderful.

Day 5: Make a note of how you interact with others. Have you changed? Have they? (Remember you can only change you, and when you do, you help others on their journey.)

Day 6: Create new meals and recipes. Purchase small portions of new and different foods. When you are offered unhealthy food, remind yourself that you already know what they taste like.

Day 7: **CONGRATULATIONS!** Can you believe it? You've made it to 21 days! In 21 days you can change old habits. Celebrate! Weigh yourself and make a note of the results. Be happy for any change. Don't brag or boast—stay the course. You've come a long way but you still have 11 months and one week to go. You will become more and more balanced as you go. You may want to check in with your physician or naturo-path for a check-up.

Week Five

Day 1: Write out the changes you feel and see in yourself. Make a note of the comments others have made. Begin to log what you are eating. Also make a note of the foods and snacks you turned down. At the end of the day, add up the approximate amount of calories you've skipped. Yeah!

Day 2: By now you are craving exercises. Cool, but-wait it out. Your body is still adjusting to the changes in eating. Make sure you have a sol-id foundation before you begin to rebuild your house. Eat your meals and drink your water.

Day 3:When you skip meals, you will crave. Do not go without and feel free to eat in front of others.

Make sure you eat. As others start to notice the change in you, you will be tempted to skip meals to speed up the process to lose more weight. **You *will* see results but they will be short-lived.** Remember, if you lose weight too fast, you will gain it back quickly. These quick, short changes will cause harm to your metabolic system. Keep eating and losing weight at a steady pace.

Day 4: Keep journaling or jotting down the changes you feel. De-clutter your closet. Anything that does not fit, you must acquit---(Sorry, I had an OJ flashback.) Remove clothes that are too big. Keep only a few incentive items. The old skinny clothes are a reminder of how much weight you've gained; remove them. Give them away or take them to a consignment store. You will feel much lighter.

Day 5: It's time to flush your body; have a massage. Start looking for board certified therapists that know how to work on a person your size. If you don't feel comfortable disrobing completely, wear a thin pair of pajamas until you do. Keep eating—don't skip meals, drink your water, laugh and love yourself.

Day 6: Eat, drink water and reassess. What foods or beverages do you still need to let go of—be honest with yourself and love you.

Day 7: Weigh yourself and celebrate. You should see a slight increase in the amount of weight loss. Massage helps regulate the stress fighting hormone cortisol which if too high or too low, causes an increase in weight. Yahoo!

Month 2: Co-Creation
Week Five

Day 1: Write out what you what you need to do today. Pay attention to how much "stuff" you are taking on from others. When others try to engage you in activities that are not on your list, politely refuse and get back to the business of your wellness.

Day 2: Start watching stretching and walking DVDs. You will not begin exercising for another week, but you can start your research now.

Day 3: How would you like to look, feel, be? Create a dream board or write out a detailed description of the self you are co-creating. Eat your six meals, drink water and dream.

Day 4: How are you feeling? Begin to identify your new comfort food. Does it trigger cravings, old memories? If so, reduce/remove. You deserve this time for you.

Day 5: Start thinking about the kinds of exercise you'd like to do and the times that would work best for you. I know you are anxious to start—not yet, but remember, preparation beats willpower.

Day 6: Have you had your weekly massage? Make sure you do. Keep eating, drinking water, and loving yourself.

Day 7: Weigh yourself and rejoice. Five weeks of healthy living looks good on you. Note the changes you have made. Reward yourself with gifts that promote wellness, like skin care products, facials, or a new yoga mat. You may even want to purchase an inexpensive piece of jewelry or some other item that can be used to encourage you. I wore a Turkish Nazar bracelet, believed in ancient times to ward off thoughts of envy and jealousy. I wore it as a reminder against comparing myself to others.

Week Six: Time to Move

Day 1: Okay, okay, you've actually been craving exercise, can you believe it? Now you get to move your body. Start with small movements with low intensity, like stretching or walking exercises. If you start out too intense, you will have no place to go. Over time you can increase your activity but start slowly so you don't burn out.

Day 2: Dance, walk or stretch for 5 minutes in the middle of your day. You may want to simply put on music and dance, park your car further from a building you frequent, or bend and stretch at your desk. Movement and exercise will help you get more oxygen to your heart and cells so your body can heal itself and keep you well. Keep eating, drinking water, loving you and moving your body.

Day 3: How are you sleeping? Now that you are moving and eating, you should be sleeping even better. Add relaxing oils to your bath and remember to turn the TV off two hours before bedtime. Find a good book. I've written a few (self-promotion is so tacky.) Make a note of your sleep patterns, how long and how well, you've rested. You need to get 7 to 8 hours of sleep each night. When you are asleep, your brain and body are at work to get you well, so get to sleep. Eat, drink your water, love you more and rest.

Week Six

Day 4: Time to de-clutter again. Pick another area at your home, work, volunteer space and your mind, and get rid of old baggage. While you are removing things, start working on that layer of dead skin. It's time to exfoliate. Purchase the necessary scrubs and a buffer. Shed that old skin. How is your body feeling? Do you notice more or fewer aches? Don't forget your weekly massage.

Day 5: Increase your movement to 10 minutes or more but don't go over 30 minutes. Create the image of the self you want to project and take five minutes thinking/meditating about it. Eat, drink water, move, love yourself and sing.

Day 6: Reorganize your kitchen around *your* needs. What can you get rid of? Make a note of what needs to go. Find new recipes and new ways to mix up your meals. Move, dance, love yourself.

Day 7: Rest and remember 6 days of exercise, one day of rest. You made it through your first week of exercising and it felt good. Weigh yourself and marvel at the new you. Plan your meals for your new week and enjoy a good night's sleep.

Week Seven: Increase of Movement

Day 1: Begin to increase your movement routine. Try something new. You will require a warm up and cool down (this should occur within your 30 minute routine.) On days when life is too hectic to stop for 30 minutes, break up the routine to 5 or 10 minute intervals. Remember; sitting is hard on to the body, get up and move.

Day 2: Don't forget to get a massage. Let your therapist know that you are moving more. Make a note of how the exercise/movement is affecting your sleep. You should be sleeping better, if not, try changing the exercise times to a different time of day and don't forget to take a hot relaxing bath and treat yourself to a hot tea before you turn in for the evening.

Day 3: How has your appetite changed? When I was doing my Wellness plan on this day I laughed about no longer liking bread. Before, I loved it so much I thought about marrying it. Make a note of the things you no longer desire. Reward yourself with something other than food.

Day 4: **Facial reminder.** Facials help reduce stress. (Every parent knows how to clinch their teeth while talking). As you lose weight, you will need to prevent your facial skin from sagging. A good facial will help. Also begin to find good skin care products that work for your skin.

Day 5: How is your water consumption? Make sure you have continued to drink water. Begin to reduce/remove other beverages and replace them with water as well. Carbonated and caffeine beverages sweetened with sugar and artificial sweeteners will begin to taste too sweet. Continue to re-train your palate.

Day 6: Don't forget your weekly massage and visualization exercise. Try doing both at the same time. If you are pressed for time, get a 10 minute chair massage. Also, call your local massage school and ask for the names of the best students. Therapists in training are required to get a certain number of hours of training before they can get their license. The cost is as low as $25 to $35 per hour.

Day 7: YAHOO! You are still on your plan and getting better every day. Weigh yourself and rejoice.

Week Eight:

Day 1: This is the day for becoming a mirror for others. Compliment someone on how they make you feel. The more you give the more you get back. Remember, eat all your meals and drink all your water. Move!

Day 2: Begin to increase the intensity of your movements. (Avoid pain; remember that nothing that heals the body should hurt the body.)

Day 3: Change the time you exercise to see if later or earlier works better for you. Smile, journal, read, and learn new ways to be a better you.

Day 4: What's eating you? Reflect back to your first week. Are the issues that affected you in the past still affecting you today? What can you do to change? Eat, drink water, move, exfoliate your skin, and sleep.

Day 5: What are others saying about you? Have they noticed a difference? If not, don't worry, I had lost a tremendous amount of weight before any-one said anything--- encourage yourself and pass it on.

Day 6: Are you moving daily? An effective habit is one you will continue throughout your life. If you don't like your routine now, you won't do it later. Find something you do enjoy.

Day 7: Rest— no movement today. Weigh yourself and smile. Make a note of how you are sleeping.

Month 3

This is the beginning of your third month and you still love yourself. Use the month to review the first three months:

Fine-tune your program. How can you be more efficient with the cost, packing and eating of meals?

I discovered that in some coffee shops the water is more filtered than bottled water, so when traveling, I carry my own water bottle and get it filled for 50 cents instead of buying it for three dollars. I also dehydrate my own fruits. It's much more cost effective.

Are you getting massaged regularly? Make sure this is a regular part of your program.

Are you drinking all of your water? Two full glasses every morning and a glass after every meal.

Are you sleeping? Sleep helps with weight loss.

Who do you need to forgive? Who do you need to be forgiven by?

Do you need to forgive yourself for anything?

Release and be free.

Exfoliate and moisturize your skin regularly. I do it at least 4 times a week. What works for you?

Month 4

Add meditation and more creative visualization.

Become even more efficient with packing and eating your six meals.

Increase your movement to 30 minutes twice a day.

Buy new clothes but don't spend too much---go to resale shops and the closets of friends because you'll soon have to replace these clothes as well.

Celebrate yourself.

Start to listen to music that uplifts.

Go dancing.

How is your eating, drinking, sleeping and play? How can you be even better?

Month 5

Re-evaluate. Look for ways to make YOUR program better.

Repeat what you did in the first month, adjusting for what works for you. This is *your* year to *your* wellness.

Month 6

Keep going. Don't think you've arrived, don't listen when people say you've lost enough weight. The program is about getting well and staying well. Remember, wellness is the alignment of the spirit mind and body. Make sure you are feeding all three. Learn new things, fuel and care for your body and feed your spirit with people and activities that create peace and joy.

What areas of your life need improvement?

What can you do to improve your situation?

What activities, people, or events do you need to let go of?

How has your health changed?

Month 7

Continue eating, exercising and loving you. Forgive yourself and others and be grateful for all that you are accomplishing.

Remove the left-over's from your life.

De-clutter your house.

Month 8

The gap between knowledge and wisdom is your ability to teach what you have learned to someone else. What have you learned and who would you like to teach? Identify those who could benefit from what you have learned and start to share. When you become the teacher, it helps to crystallize what you have learned.

Month 9

Reassess your program. Are there still foods that you need to eliminate or reduce? Have you been drinking enough water? Are you resting well at night? How is your attitude? Remember, this program is not just about losing weight, it's about being well, in spirit, mind and body. The more you fine tune your program, the more fine-tuned you will become.

Redo reflections and exercises from chapters 4, 6 and 7. How do your answers differ from when you first started your Wellness plan? How can you do better? (Don't try to speed the weight loss, you are doing great—stay the course it takes a year.)

Month 10

Change meals and exercises. Make your program even better. Relax and celebrate all of the accomplishments. Make a list of the things you can do better.

Month 11

How has your life improved?

How have your eating habits improved since you started your Wellness plan?

Are you sleeping more soundly and peacefully?

How do you feel about your overall health?

How has your exercise and movements changed for you? How is your posture and body alignment? Be conscious of standing straighter and taller. Push your shoulders back, raise your head and breathe. Practice improving your posture in a mirror.

How have your significant relationships changed?

Month 12

Congratulations, you have reached month twelve! Have you achieved your desired outcomes? When I reached my last month, I had lost more weight than I anticipated, but my goal had changed. I no longer fretted about numbers on a scale, the size I wore, or about being able to fit into clothes made by someone who didn't have me in mind when they made them. My intentions and aspirations were about the way I felt and moved and coexisted with others and my surroundings.

I secretly decided that what I wanted more than anything was to perform a dance, just one dance in front of a live audience.

When I was an undergraduate student, I studied choreography. I had a brilliant instructor who had been a student of Martha Graham. I loved my dance class and the way I felt afterward. I was the only fat girl in a class with long, lean men and women who had studied for years. My desire to learn was so intense, that my instructor was always happy to see me and graciously spent extra time encouraging me despite my size. When I lost weight that summer of undergrad, she encouraged me to perform, but I refused. Even though I was much smaller than I'd been and almost the size of the other students, I still felt and moved like a big person. Friends had to remind me that I could now stand with my feet together, or that I should pull my shoulders back. When I danced though, my body felt free from the burdens, mental and physical of being fat. Still, I refused to dance in public.

It was not until the twelfth month of my wellness plan that I mentioned to the meeting planners of a conference at which I'd be speaking, that I wanted to perform a dance. The conference, National Training Institute for the American Association of Critical

Care Nurses is an event where thousands of critical care nurses gather to learn even more about the incredible work they do and to celebrate their achievements. When I mentioned to them that I'd always wanted to perform a dance, the organizers Dana and Lisa, informed me that I would be doing it at the conference.

In May of 2010, my dream came true when I performed a dance in front of 8,000 critical care nurses.

I still tear up at the very thought of it.

Just one year before, my body ached from the illnesses and diseases that plagued me. At that time, I was physically and emotionally drained, but after just twelve short months on my Wellness plan, I was energized and renewed.

At the end of my short but powerful dance, the audience jumped to their feet and erupted with applause. The nurses rushed up afterwards to tell me how inspired they were by my dance and how they knew they could be well, too.

Your goals and dreams are for you, but when you become better, you light a pathway for others around you.

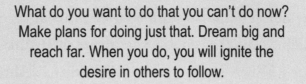

What do you want to do that you can't do now?
Make plans for doing just that. Dream big and
reach far. When you do, you will ignite the
desire in others to follow.

How would you like to feel in one year?

Create your own wellness plan for just one week
to start and take it day by day.

Keep a journal of your new eating, sleeping, exercise and thinking habits. This will be extremely necessary when you start out as you are replacing old well-established habits.

Set intentions and aspirations for what you'd like to be able to do. Do you want to perform a dance in public, walk on the beach in a bathing suit, or maybe just sit in a movie theatre without eating popcorn? Your intentions and aspirations are for you; they can never be too small or too great.

What would you like to let go of?

How do you feel at this moment, right now?

Notes

"When you walk with Purpose,
you collide with Destiny"

A Year to Wellness

Chapter Fourteen

Pass It On

*"Learning is finding out what we already know.
Doing is demonstrating that you know it. Teaching is
reminding others that they know just as well as you."*
—*Author, Richard Bach*

ONCE YOU'VE APPLIED THE TECHNIQUES OF YOUR
Year to Wellness Plan and have experienced the results,
you must share your wisdom with someone else. By
passing on what you have learned, you are reinforcing
the lessons for yourself.

After Mary had lost one hundred pounds, she
began to share her lessons with her sister. Mary says
that there were some days when she felt like giving
up, but then her sister would call to discuss her own
challenges or success stories and Mary would find
the encouragement *she* needed.

The South African philosophy of *Ubuntu* stresses the belief that an individual becomes more human and humane as they connect to others. In other words, a person is a person through other persons. The idea that "I am because we are" becomes critical for your wellness. By connecting to others who are also in need of wellness you are creating a cycle of well-being.

Gratitude is also necessary in being whole and complete. There is a story in the Bible where Jesus Christ heals ten lepers. Only one leper returns to say thank you. To the one who has returned, Jesus rhetorically asks, "Weren't there nine more?" Then he says to the sole returnee, "Because of your faith you have been made whole." All of them were healed but only the one who returned in gratitude was made whole.

Gratitude completes us; it completes the cycle of giving and receiving. When you share what you know with others you strengthen your own transformation.

Because of the complexity of the program, you should start to help or encourage just one person at a time. When others begin to notice your transformation and start asking what you are doing, make sure you are well into the program yourself; at least six to nine months. Identify someone whose struggles are similar to your own. This person is someone who cares more for others than they do themselves, who has tried numerous diets, pills and weight loss programs and is struggling with issues of self-esteem.

Do not take on more than you can bear. You are not a coach or mentor, simply someone who is sharing what they have learned. You will be tempted to shout from the rooftops, but avoid the desire to boast or brag about your results. You will get a sense or feeling of whom you should be assisting on their journey.

Once you have identified this person, create a schedule for conversing about the program. During their first three months, try to chat at least once a week, but no more. This Wellness program allows each individual to co-create the plan they will need. Make sure that the person you assist works at creating their own plan, rather than trying to duplicate yours.

I have also given small presents to those I have assisted. When Sally made the breakthrough of giving up her trigger food, I presented her with a pedometer for later in the program when she started her walking routine. I gave another woman a journal and Mary received a week at a spa (I was working there, so it was free.)

No good deed goes unrewarded. As I have reached out to others, I've received so much in return. I've gotten calls from spa directors inviting me to come in for treatments, massage therapists have provided me with their services pro bono, and authors have sent books and articles "just because." We've all heard the adage, "What goes around, comes around." When you do an act of kindness for someone, kindness comes back, especially when you are not expecting it.

Chapter Fifteen

Review and Renew

"People, even more than things, have to be restored,
renewed, received, reclaimed and redeemed;
never throw out anyone."

—*Actress and Humanitarian, Audrey Hepburn*

WHEN YOU LOOK OVER YOUR *YEAR TO WELLNESS PLAN*, you will notice many things. Among them is the fact that the year, though challenging at times and exhilarating at others, went by relatively quickly. I recently got a call from a friend who had taken pictures of me the week I started my wellness plan. He had seen me during the year and was always amazed by my results each time he saw me, but when he looked back at pictures from just one year prior, he could not believe what he was seeing.

"I took those pictures," he exclaimed. "You didn't

look this big though," he said.

Even though he had seen me at 290 pounds, his mind would not accept that I had actually been that big. The present me had erased the previous image of me from his memories of what I had looked like. He also commented on just how quickly it happened. I laughed and told him that's why the program is called *A Year to Wellness*—because it takes a year.

When some people first hear that they will have to commit a year to the program, they often respond that this is too much time. These people want big re-sults and fast, but the best results come gradually, in small bites. This way the impact is much longer last-ing. You will find that the year moves faster than you anticipated. You will also realize that your new habits have replaced the old ones.

After working on my health, I wanted to work on other aspects of myself. I began a year of finan-cial wellness; de-cluttering my life of old ways and replacing them with fiscally healthy habits. What would you like to improve: a relationship, your emo-tional health, or your parenting skills? Give yourself a year and set out a course to be better day by day, month by month and year by year.

Celebrate

Go on a trip or discover a great place in your own hometown. Renovate, plant a garden or a tree. Start attending local, free lectures and museum openings. Reward yourself with the life you didn't even know you could have. As I've mentioned before, people often celebrate the success of weight loss with high calorie foods and beverages. This is not only unhealthy but it will send you back on the same maddening rollercoaster you've devoted a year to get off of. When you celebrate, and you must, do so with the people who are also working at improving themselves.

Surround Yourself with Healthy People

It is critical that you surround yourself with people who have a positive outlook. If you are around those who are constantly complaining, you will soon find things to complain about. A negative energy cannot abide with a positive one, it will change or leave. When you encounter negativity, raise your energy and become even more positive.

See Yourself as New

Remember, others will have a hard time believing your transformation. They will only see the new you and will not have an accurate picture of how far you have come. In contrast, you may have a difficult time thinking that you have come far enough. Too often, people who have lost weight begin to fixate on individual areas that are not yet toned or are larger than others. Please don't do that to yourself. Instead remind yourself daily of how wonderful you are, were and always will be. Look at how far you've come and continue confidently on your journey.

Look at your pictures from a year ago. How has your appearance changed? (Be specific and detailed: e.g., eyes, skin, hair texture and sheen, etc.)

How have your attitude, outlook and overall wellbeing changed in one year?

As a result of your transformation, how
have others changed?

What area in your life would you like to work on next?

Start creating a wellness plan for that area by reading
and researching as much as possible.

Begin to outline your new wellness plan.
What would your first week look like?

Notes

**"When you walk with Purpose,
you collide with Destiny"**

Chapter Sixteen

Live

"The secret of health for both mind and body is not the future, but to live the present moment wisely and earnestly."

—*Buddha*

THROUGHOUT THE DURATION AND AFTER THE COMpletion of your *Year to Wellness*, practice staying focused on the present. Live from day to day and celebrate the moment you are in now. Time goes by whether we are consciously engaged in life or not. When you are engaged and active in the process of change, you are in control.

Live each day more fully than you did the day before. Seek new ideas, new roads, new friends, new music and a new song.

When I started becoming more and more well, I had the tendency to think "What if? What if I'd done this sooner?" and "What if I had known it was this easy before?" I would sometimes fantasize about a life free from mistakes and uninformed choices. Then one day, it occurred to me that I still had the rest of my life to live with the new information I'd learned, and that by applying and living fully, I could ignite the passion in others to do the same. I knew that my children and all the children I influenced would have the opportunity to learn from the missteps of my life and create their own paths.

Be open to the change and opportunities that come to you. Allow the lessons you are learning to inspire you in your career, education, community involvement, family, and other aspects of your life. Try new things and see how they work for you. Just as you have maintained old ideas about weight loss and wellness, you have also harbored false ideas about the world in general.

I have grown in so many ways.

I have learned to listen even when I don't want to with the expectation that I am always learning something new.

I am much calmer and worry much less.

I forgive more easily and am learning to let go of

my need to be needed. (Though my children may tell you otherwise.)

I no longer see a need to change or fix anyone else as I understand that I can only change myself.

I love more, cling less and let go when it's time to.

I am hopeful, expectant and always believing that I can make the world a better place by becoming a better person.

"Be the change you want to see in the world"
—Ghandi

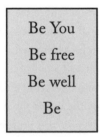

Be You
Be free
Be well
Be

Notes

The following notes and references will provide you with additional information and reference material for your *Year to Wellness*.

Introduction and Chapter One

The NPR radio interview with Michelle Martin was on Tell Me More and can be heard online at http://www.npr.org/templates/story/story.php?storyId=126285591.

The words "fat" and "adiposity" are used instead of "overweight" of "obese." Obese is a medical condition which views fat, any fat, as problematic. Overweight implies that a person is over an idealized weight. We fail to understand and embrace the notion of weight diversity. We are not all made to be thin. Yet, the height and weight charts present idealized expectations for entire populations. These weight charts were created by insurance companies based on where we should all be if we were all the same. But we are all unique beings; some fat, some thin, some in between. We can be healthy while fat or sick while thin, yet there is an expectation and a cultural standard of beauty that dictates that we all are thin or try to get there.

"Thin" was not always the norm for Americans. Prior to the 1920's, fat was equal to beauty and prosperity. (Fraser, 2010) However, as more and more immigrants flooded in to the United States from poor European countries, the elite wanted to distinguished themselves from the shorter, rounder immigrants.(ibid, 2010) Weight became a measure of class distinction, hence the idea that one could never be too thin or too rich. For an excellent collection of studies on weight discrimination you <u>must</u> read *The Fat Studies Reader* by Esther D. Rothblum, Sondra Solovay, 2009.

Diets don't work. To find out more go to http://magazine.

ucla.edu/exclusives/dieting_no-go/.

My brother Kevin recently retired after 32 years in the marines. He is, once again my ace, my sidekick, my cheerleader. To find out more about the Slim America Weight Loss Project go to slimamericaweightlossproject.com.

Chapter Two

In this chapter I discuss diet plans and gym programs that did not work for me. For a great study on the marketing of the weight loss industry, see the Federal Trade Commissions' report on Weight Loss Advertising: An analysis of Current Trends at http://www.ftc.gov/bcp/reports/weightloss.pdf.

Chapter Three

I was not the only casualty of the kickball tournament. The next day, and for several more, I received lots of calls from folks who had to stay home from work to recuperate from the game. I still have family fun activities, but they are more sensible and appropriate to the skills of my non-athletic friends.

Chapter Four

For additional information on how Cortisol levels and stress affect the body, read Elizabeth Scott's article on stress management at http://stress.about.com/od/stress health/a/cortisol. htm.

Chapter Five

Dr. Steven Hobby is a pediatrician in Savannah, Georgia and works with the Children's Pediatrics Care Center. He also volunteers his services for children of international adoptions and has assisted in over 400 adoptions.

My daughter Fatima, now 18, says she never wants to leave

her pediatrician and is writing a vampire book about a recent hematological illness she suffered and Dr. Hobby, the vampire slayer.

Mark Armstrong has a naturopathic care center in Atlanta, Georgia. To learn more about his practice, go to *www.ahimki. net.*

Chapter Six
Read more about cellular rejuvenation by Michael Staub at *www.ehow.com* and search rejuvenate cells.

For an excellent study in weight discrimination, read *The Study on Weight Bias: The Need for Public Policy by Rudd Center for Food Policy & Obesity.* Yale University, 2008.

Chapter Seven
To find out more about your metabolism read the article in Pub Med Central titled, Muscle oxidative metabolism accelerates with mild acidosis during incremental intermittent isometric plantar flexion exercise by Homma et, al or just trust me. For more information, on Red Mountain Resort and Spa in Utah, go to *www.redmountainspa.com* and tell them Bertice sent you.

Chapter Eight
I would tell you how to find Garrett's Popcorn, but I don't want to turn you on to the habit I've only recently kicked.

For a list of possible trigger foods and their side effects go to www. helpforibs.com (ibs = irritable bowel system).

What inspires you? Find a saying or quote and have it made into jewelry. My editor, Janet Hill, now runs a company called On This Rock NYC which designs beautiful, inspirational pieces. Janet made bracelet for me with my saying, When You Walk with Purpose, You Collide with Destiny. Whenever I looked down at it, I was able to remind myself that by doing daily habits of purpose, I would find my destiny. To learn more about Janet's wonderful pieces, go to www.onthisrocknyc.com.

Chapter Nine
Dr. Howard Murad's Inclusive Health Center is located in El Segundo, California. Visitors will experience the Murad Method Program for improving topical, internal and emotional health based on the science of Cellular Water Principal.
For a more in depth discussion of Bennett and Gurin's Set Point Theory go to *www.weightlossforall.com* and search under body fat storage.

Chapter Eleven
In this chapter I present tips that are essential to your wellness. After much trial and error, on myself and others, I have found these ingredients to be an integral part of your well being.

Hydration Therapy: There is a great deal of debate around water; bottle vs. plastic, distilled vs. spring and on and on. The most important thing is that you drink water. Avoid those who comment on the type, amount or times you should drink water and just drink it.

Massage: Once you start getting massages, you will find it difficult to stop. If you are not accustomed to having massage, allow yourself to become comfortable. Start with a chair massage and disrobe to the level of your comfort. Massage will help you on your journey.

Sleep, Skin Exfoliation and Moisturizing: There are numerous natural products available to help improve your sleep and to exfoliate and moisturize your skin. I have deliberately not endorsed any here. I have my favorites and you will have yours. What works for me may not work for you. I have tried products that do nothing for me but find that they work small miracles for my daughter. There is no one product that works for everybody. Find out what works for you.

Visualization: When I was just 12, my sister Myrna gave me a copy of *Science of the Mind* by Ernest Holmes. I cried because I wanted a bike. Now, at 50, this book is a treasure trove. Purchase a copy and take the time to ingest it. Also read *Message of A Master* by John McDonald. The exercises in this small book had a huge impact on wellness, relationships and even my finances. Read Dan Millman's *Way of The Peaceful Warrior* and see the movie *Peaceful Warrior* with someone you love. You'll be so glad you did.

Chapter Twelve

Check out the power of laughter at www.guidetolaughing.com, David J Pollay's *Law of The Garbage Truck* at www.bewareofgarbagetrucks.com and your local United Way, homeless shelter, shelter for battered women, hospital volunteer board, after school program or any place you can channel your energy. The more you channel your energy into something positive, the less time you will have for focusing on the negative.

Remember this is your year to wellness. Avoid comparing yourself to others. Find out what works for you and stick with it. Share what you have learned but allow others to learn for them. Remember, the only person you can change is you.

At the end of this section, I wrote about performing a dance for the American Association of Critical Care Nurses. Critical care nurses are amazing individuals. At some point in your life, you will encounter them; either caring for you or someone you love. After watching the care of my mother, I learned how essential they are in our lives, yet too often, they go unappreciated. If you know one (and chances are you do) thank them for their service to the country.

Chapter Thirteen

In this chapter I discuss the need to "pass it on". You will be amazed by the power of sharing what you've learned with someone else. Everyday I have the opportunity to touch someone's life with a kind word, thought or deed. Compliment, encourage, uplift and share your joy with others; you will be so much better for it.

Additional Resources

For information on the Metabolism
http://www.thatsfit.com/
http://www.nlm.nih.gov/medlineplus/metabolic syndrome.html
http://www.articlesbase.com/fitness-articles/how-to-speed-up-a-slow-
metabolism-179763.html

For information on Weight Bias
http://www.naafaonline.com/dev2/about/Brochures/Weight
BiasPolicyRuddReport.pdf
http://www.ncbi.nlm.nih.gov/pubmed/8014833
http://www.nature.com/oby/journal/v15/n3/full/oby200784a.
html
http://www.ncbi.nlm.nih.gov/pubmed/8014833

For information on the Benefits of Massage
http://ezinearticles.com/?Weight-Loss-Benefits-of-
Massage&id=33223

For information on the Relationship between
Cortisol and Stress
http://stress.about.com/od/stresshealth/a/cortisol.htm

For information on Childhood Obesity
http://www.suite101.com/content/childhood-overweight-of
ten-goes-undiagnosed-a87447

For information on Food Addictions and Trigger Foods
http://www.suite101.com/content/a-new-gene-nrxn3-is-asso
ciated-to-obesity-a129559

http://health.yahoo.net/experts/drmao/what-soft-drinks-ar`e-doing-
your-body
http://www.nutramed.com/eatingdisorders/addictive
foods.htm

For information on the Link between Obesity and Diabetes
http://www.elements4health.com/study-discovers-link-
between-obesity-and-diabetes.html

For information on Exercise
http://smallstepstohealth.com/2009/08/effects-exercise/
http://www.mayoclinic.com/health/exercise/
HQ01676/NSECTIONGROUP=2

For information on Cellular Rejuvenation
http://www.ehow.com/how_5047804_rejuvenate-cells html

For information on The Set Point Theory
http://www.weightlossforall.com/body-fat-set-point.htm

Bibliography

Allen, James. *As A Man Thinketh* New York: DeVorss Publication, 1948

Allen, James. *The Way of Peace* Hard Press, 2006

Besant, Annie Word and Charles Webster Leadbeter. *Thought Forms* Los Angeles, CA Indo European Publishing, 2010

Finer, Evan. *Effortless Well being: The Missing Ingredients for Authentic Wellness*: Lake Zurich, IL Well being Resources, 2003

Hall, Manly P. *The Secret Teachings of All Ages. An Encyclopedic Outline of Masonic, Hermetic, Qabbalistic and Rosicrucian Symbolical Philosophy* forgotten books.org 1928 republished 2008

Hawkins, David R. *Power vs. Force: The Hidden Detriments of Human Behavior* Carlsbad, CA: Hay House 1995

Hicks, Ester and Jerry Hicks. *The Astonishing Power of Emotions* New York: Hay House Carlsbad, CA 2007

Holmes, Ernest. *The Science of the Mind* New York: G.P. Putman's Sons 1938

Kress, Diane. *The Metabolism Miracle: 3 Easy Steps to Regain Control of Your Weight...Permanently* Philadelphia Da Capo Press, 2009

Lawrence, Brother. *The Practice of The Presence of God* Christian Books Today, 1999

Lin, Linda and Kathleen Reid. *The Relationship Between Media Exposure and Antifat Attitudes: The Role of Dysfunctional Appearance Beliefs Body Images*, Vol.6. Issue 1, January, 2009 Pages 52-55

Millman, Dan. *Way of the Peaceful Warrior: A Book That Changes Lives* H.J. Kramer: New World Library, 2000

McTaggert. *The International Experiment: Using Your Thoughts to*

Change Your Life and the World New York: Free Press, 2007

Rama, Rudolph Ballentine and Alan Hynes. *Science of Breath: A Practical Guide* Honesdale, PA: The Himalayan Institute Press, 1979

Roach, Michael. *The Tibetan Book of Yoga: Ancient Buddhist Teachings on the Philosophy and Practice of Yoga* New York, Random House, 2009

Rothblum, Ester and Sandra Solovay, ed. *The Fat Studies Reader* New York: New York University Press, 2009

Shainburg, Catherine. *Kabbalah and The Power of Dreaming: Awakening The Visionary Life* Rochester, Vermont Inner Traditions, 2005

Trine, Ralph Waldo. *The Higher Power of Mind and Spirit London*: G. Bell and Sons, LTD, 1918

Walport, Stuart. *Dieting Doesn't Work* UCLA Magazine April, 2007